# Praise for Splash!

"*Splash!* is a captivating and inspirational book that shines a light on the lives of young women in rural India who courageously challenge gender norms. Through captivating storytelling, Rekha takes us on a journey into the struggles and triumphs of these resilient girls as they break free from societal constraints. *Splash!* is a testament to the power of determination and the human spirit, offering valuable insights into the lives of those who dare to defy expectations. This book is a must-read for anyone seeking inspiration and a deeper understanding of the pursuit of dreams in the face of adversity."

—**Dr. Marshall Goldsmith,** Thinkers50 #1 executive coach and *New York Times* best-selling author of *The Earned Life, Triggers,* and *What Got You Here Won't Get You There*

"Of the 22,000 girls who embarked on journeys with PANI over the past eight years, *Splash!* illuminates the stories of girls who dared to swim upstream in Uttar Pradesh, a persistent patriarchal stronghold where many families still mourn the birth of girls as lifelong burdens. The girls share snippets of daily 15-kilometer bike rides, peddling through the ranks of harassing boys, jeering men, gossipmongers, disapproving and, at times, abusive kin. And that was just to get to the resource centres that would connect them to their dreams. Steadfast, they pushed through barriers to join male-dominated sectors, such as sports, chauffeuring, and welding and to transform male bastions, such as the army, police, and border security forces, making them more accessible to women seeking their services. This collection of heartfelt, personal stories spotlights the young women's resoluteness and resourcefulness as they uplifted their families and served to inspire girls in their villages and beyond to 'bravely walk down untrodden paths.' Through their own words and wrapped in Rekha Saleela Nair's fecund turns of phrase, the book nurtures and nuances our own grasp of how seemingly everyday patterns can be the very shackles and aspiration-gutters of girls, whether in underserved communities in Northern India or innumerable other contexts."

—**Tzili Mor,** MSc, JD, LLM, advisor, strategist, and legal practitioner for global gender justice and human rights; former director of Georgetown Law and International Women's Human Rights Clinic; deputy director of CARE's Global Policy and Advocacy

"Rekha provides captivating portraits of young women who were supported by People's Action for National Integration (PANI) in rural India to overcome rigid gender roles so they could grow and build lives that were meaningful to them. With PANI, she went into eastern Uttar Pradesh to develop trust with these young warriors who told their stories to her. These touched my heart and provided a view of life, caste, and gender issues I had not fully understood. I believe that you will be both moved and informed."

—**Jordan Goldrich,** member of 100 Coaches, ACEC, PCC, executive coach, speaker, best-selling author

"Rekha provides insights into the human condition that can only be gained by living and working among those who have the least. Working with the nonprofit group PANI, Rekha has been able to capture the journeys of young women in Uttar Pradesh as they asserted themselves to achieve better and more fulfilled lives. *Splash!* is a work that will make you feel good about how individuals can make a positive difference even in the most challenging situations."

—**John Baldoni,** member of 100 Coaches, keynote speaker, and author of many books on leadership, including *Grace Under Pressure: Leading Through Change and Crisis*

"Vandana, Kajal, Shivani are role models—girls who have faced and overcome incredible challenges in their lives. From poverty and violence to discrimination and abuse, these girls have shown tremendous strength and resilience in the face of adversity and are an inspiration to us all. The role of PANI and that of a place to call their 'own' shines through in this wonderful compilation by Rekha. *Splash!* is a celebration of adolescent girls' strength and resilience and is a must-read for parents, educators, and anyone else who works with girls."

—**Shivani Gupta,** co-CEO, The Womanity Foundation

"*Splash!* is a book worth reading for anyone who believes there are big problems that seem unsolvable, challenges that seem impossible to overcome, and barriers that seem insurmountable. Such experiences lead one to feel despair and helplessness. Rekha's book shows a path to dispelling such thoughts and feelings with true story after true story of overcoming unbelievable challenges, breaking through impenetrable barriers, and solving those unsolvable problems. This book inspires us to have the hope, courage, and confidence to build a much better world where we all can make the needed changes to live a better, more fulfilling life."

—**Frank Wagner,** co-creator of Stakeholder Centered Coaching®

"*Splash!* is a great reminder of when we give the brains back to people, they achieve glorious and useful accomplishments. This illustrative depiction of strong and capable girls and women in rural India who defied the odds to be exemplars to disenfranchised women everywhere is well written and insightful."

—**Bill Flynn,** member of 100 Coaches, author, and speaker

"These remarkable stories spring from living examples of transformative changes brought about by mutual interactions of individual agency of adolescent girls with the social processes that challenge the gendered social norms. I have personally engaged with PANI and met many of the heroes of these stories to learn firsthand about their travails and triumphs in greatly challenging social conditions. It is a testimony to the long and grounded work by PANI that ordinary individuals could show exceptional ingenuity and tenacity to overcome age-old social barriers. They have made a difference to their own lives as well as to the lives of many others by their examples. I am sure these stories will inspire many more real and potential change agents."

—**Kanchan Sinha,** former country director, Oxfam Tanzania

"*Splash!* offers us powerful examples of the role culture plays in shaping an individual's frame of reference and how young people develop unconscious life scripts that are compliant with the cultural frame of reference of the societies in which they grow up. In Transactional Analysis, a frame of reference is understood to be the way people define things and events in their lives and how to act in response to those definitions. Life scripts are unconscious life plans that are a part of an individual's frame of reference. The stories in this book are sensitively narrated. They take us through the journeys of young women in rural India, and even men in certain narratives, who make new decisions that liberate them from their scripts, update their frame of reference, and allow new ego-states to emerge. *Splash!* shows us how honoring the essence of human beings with an 'I'm OK/You're OK' attitude can enable a deeper understanding of behaviours that may be problematic and facilitate transformation. My thanks to Rekha for opening my eyes to how this plays out in a cultural setting I have not studied."

—**Wayne Hart, PhD,** psychologist, founder, Transactional Analysis Now | TA-Now, Certified Teaching and Supervising Transactional Analyst (ITAA), Transactional Analysis Practitioner Instructor (USATAA/NAATA), Senior Fellow, Center for Creative Leadership

"As the father of two adolescent girls, I found myself deeply moved by the journeys of the young women that have been captured in detail and poignantly narrated by Rekha in *Splash!* When young girls are nurtured with dignity, granted access to education, and treated as equals, society as a whole progresses. This seminal work shows us the power of small, righteous actions taken in seemingly impossible situations that add up slowly to create an equitable community for our daughters and sons alike. The stories in this book show us how we can pave the way for future generations to thrive in a just community where all are valued. The onus falls on each of us to take our cues from the stories; to speak out and stand up for the rights and well-being of girls and women everywhere."

—**Mahesh M. Thakur,** member of 100 Coaches, keynote speaker

"The stories contained in this book are stories of courage and conviction of young girls from rural areas who dared to break social restrictions and defy prescriptive roles. With the help of PANI's resource centres and a dedicated cadre of mentors, the girls could relate to their dreams and give wings to their aspirations. From welder Aarti to cricketer Antima to defence personnel Vandana and kabaddi player Shivani, each story is a living example of zeal, enthusiasm, and courage. I am sure the stories in *Splash!* will inspire everyone—young persons, development workers, politicians, academicians, researchers, and the general public—to embrace the limitless potential in every adolescent girl."

—**Professor Sanjai Bhatt,** University of Delhi, former president, National Association of Professional Social Workers in India

"The stories in this collection are moving and inspiring. They tell us about things we don't want to discuss and deliberately avoid. In a context where we find comfort in normalizing subordination and hierarchy under the guise of culture and norms, the stories here show that girls, particularly from the most marginalized and impoverished families, are finding paths to freedom. They are striving for freedom from injustice, oppression, discrimination, and brutal violence—in order to achieve their aspirations for a just, equal, and deserving place in society. Rekha Saleela Nair has depicted each girl's intricate and dignified journey in a way that is incredibly captivating. I sincerely applaud PANI for doing such a great job acting as a trigger and inspiring hope that these little splashes of change will become waves of it!"

—**Dr. Ravi Verma,** regional director, Asia, International Center for Research on Women (ICRW)

"Patriarchy, with its deeply embedded and often unquestionably accepted social norms, is a powerful force holding back societal-wide social and economic progress on multiple fronts. Challenging those norms and more intentionally investing in the empowerment of women and girls is increasingly viewed and justified as 'smart economics,' which it is. The stories in *Splash!* provide a more qualitative, human, and compelling case for challenging gendered social norms. Set in rural Uttar Pradesh, where the norms restricting girls are particularly extreme and entrenched, these inspiring stories of girls who had the courage and tools to fight against the strong tide of patriarchal norms demonstrate what is possible. What these brave girls have accomplished with the support of PANI provides not only inspiration, but practical wisdom for anyone seeking to challenge and overcome the deeply damaging constraints placed upon girls across the world. The yearnings of the girls in *Splash!* resonate deeply with my aspirations of freedom, justice, and opportunity for my own daughters—and for all girls."

—**Tim Hanstad,** vice chair, Chandler Foundation, co-founder, Landesa Skoll Social Entrepreneur Awardee

# Splash!

## TRUE STORIES OF GIRLS IGNITING CHANGE IN RURAL INDIA

# REKHA SALEELA NAIR

### FOR THE PEOPLE'S ACTION FOR NATIONAL INTEGRATION (PANI), INDIA

**BrainTrust**
INK

The names and identifying characteristics of persons referenced in this book have been changed to protect their privacy.

BrainTrust Ink
Nashville, Tennessee
www.braintrustink.com

Distributed by River Grove Books

Design and composition by Greenleaf Book Group
Cover design by Greenleaf Book Group
Cover images © Adobe Stock/Marina, © Adobe Stock/MicroOne, and © Adobe Stock/galyna_p

Publisher's Cataloging-in-Publication data is available.

Print ISBN: 978-1-956072-21-1

eBook ISBN: 978-1-956072-22-8

First Edition

*This book is a celebration of the indomitable spirit of the young women in the villages around Ayodhya in Uttar Pradesh, India, whose empowered choices have created splashes and ripples within their families and village communities. They have braved great odds to set the wheels of change in motion. Their journeys are a testament to the grace and power of the human spirit to rise above limitations of gender, environment, culture, and society.*

# Contents

# Foreword

The stories in *Splash!* transported me back in time to a freezing winter evening in 2000, when in Rajasthan, I attended one of my first trainings on fundamental rights. Fresh out of college and newly employed, I was engrossed in a mime presented as a part of the training, which depicted the journey of a young couple into marriage and parenthood. I was able to follow the story to the point where the woman became pregnant and gave birth, but what came after perplexed me. As I was horrified to discover, the newborn, a girl, was abandoned in the jungle by her family. It shocked me even more that everyone else watching seemed to be unperturbed, as if such actions were entirely normal. In the twenty-three years since that evening, I have travelled widely and interacted with diverse communities throughout India. I have yet to come across a society where girls are as cherished as boys are.

This Indian preference for boys is rooted in cultural and societal factors. Patrilocal marriages, in which a bride relocates to her husband's home, makes daughters transient members in their families of origin. A daughter grows up hearing that the home where she was born and raised is not her true home.

Instead, she is told that she belongs to her future marital home, wherever that may be. Sons, on the other hand, are entrusted with performing death rites of parents and therefore considered the natural heirs to the family name, assets, and legacy. Thus, from the very beginning, many daughters are deprived of one of the most fundamental human dignities, of being welcomed into the world.

In far too many places, girls are neglected as they grow up, which has adverse effects on their physical and mental well-being. They face barriers in accessing quality education, lack full legal and social rights, and struggle to acquire economic assets. A colossal bundle of discriminatory norms and beliefs consistently tell daughters that they are lesser beings, they deserve less, and they must be satisfied with less.

Since girls' inequality is rooted in culture-specific gender biases, it has a unique face in each context. Living in Uttar Pradesh, the setting for the stories in *Splash!*, I am familiar with the suffocating grip of these biases that manifest in rigid behavioural codes governing every aspect of a girl's daily life, from the way she sits to the way she talks, laughs, dresses, and even eats. These codes subtly seep into our consciousness without us being aware of it and are present in the language we speak, the books we read, the media we consume, and the music we listen to. We often accept them as unassailable, unquestionable truths.

They create a framework for the archetype of a "good girl" that grooms young girls to listen and follow meekly. Good girls do not argue. They stay inside houses. They hang their head down. They sit in shrunken postures. They do not have an opinion. In short, good girls are expected to be giving, compromising, and adjusting, so that they grow up to be devoted wives or *pativratas*, as idealised and romanticised in legends, folklore, folksongs, and through various ceremonies. The relentless pursuit of being "good" leads to the erasure of the girls' true selves. They often are unable to express their full range of emotions and struggle to identify with their own feelings. The challenge then is to help the girls realise their selfhood in full measure.

*Splash!* features the stories of adolescent girls who stand up to these rigid norms and take control of their destinies. Within these tales, young girls recount the restrictions placed upon them by their families, driven by the fear of societal scrutiny, and their own challenges in communicating their desire to play, dance, sing, study, and earn in a society that emphasises early marriage. These determined young women confront their internal conflicts and attune themselves to their emotions. They summon the bravery to speak out, support one another as they negotiate with their families and peers, carve unique paths, and emerge as exemplars for other girls.

From the Commission on the Status of Women in 1947 to the recently concluded G20 summit in New Delhi, there are a horde of conventions and declarations that recognise gender equality as not only a fundamental human right, but a necessary foundation for a peaceful, prosperous, and sustainable world. Yet we are awfully short of achieving these goals. The

2023 report on Sustainable Development Goals by the United Nations mentions that at the current rates of progress, it will take three hundred years to end child marriage and nearly as long to close gaps in legal protection. To accelerate the pace of change, it is not enough to acknowledge the existence of these biases. Rather, it is essential to confront and dismantle them.

That is exactly what these stories do. They not only draw attention to the issues and potential solutions, but also emphasise that focusing solely on sector-specific programmes, like improving health or educational attainment or mental well-being, is inadequate. Instead, girls require holistic, interconnected, and intersectional support that reflects the totality of their lived experiences. These stories also illustrate that even the most entrenched attitudes and norms can undergo transformation. They serve as a reminder that change is achievable and well within our grasp.

Adolescence marks a pivotal phase in personal development where individuals mould their identities and cultivate fundamental attitudes, values, and skills. It presents a prime opportunity to interrupt the cycle of vulnerability and generate positive change that can persist through generations. *Splash!* offers engaging accounts of the journeys of adolescent girls as they evolve from being passive observers to using their voices, asserting their choices, and taking control of their lives. They refuse to inherit the silence of their mothers, which inspires hope that future generations may inherit a more open, inclusive, and accepting world to navigate.

I hope these stories that are soulfully crafted by my friend Rekha Saleela Nair resonate with you as they did with me. Rekha has spent several hours interviewing these girls, coaxing experiences, aspirations, and stories from them in their houses, on village playgrounds, and by speaking with their mentors. She was able to connect with them at a personal level, which helped the girls, and often their family members as well, to open up and share. I hope their eloquence and courage inspire you to offer your support, not just to these girls but to all little girls around you.

One powerful act of support is to tell every girl that, no matter what, they belong to the homes and families they are born into and to affirm this pledge by ensuring that they have equal rights to the family assets and heritage. It is this infallible sense of belonging that will enable girls, in India and around the world, to share their vitality and resilience with countless others.

Witnessing girls find happiness is akin to watching the world transform into a more beautiful place. Let us hear them and give them the autonomy and strength they need to lead and thrive so that they can embark on an upward trajectory of productive and fulfilled lives.

*Shipra Deo*
*Global Gender and Land Advisor, Landesa;*
*Board Vice President, Working Group*
*for Women and Land Ownership;*
*Advisory Council Member, The Womanity Foundation*

# Preface

Forty years ago, the foundation of the People's Action for National Integration (PANI) was laid with the vision of creating inclusive societies where individuals have greater control over their life situations and can take responsibility for building a mutually rewarding world. Over the years, PANI's leadership team has steadfastly pursued this vision, tirelessly working towards positive change. While we have witnessed our interventions facilitating transformation, what has unfolded in Tarun over the past eight years has left us spellbound.

Eastern Uttar Pradesh, India, the backdrop for this journey, is a region steeped in deeply ingrained gender norms that have long stifled the aspirations of its women and girls. These rigidly defined gender roles not only curtail women and girl's mobility, education, and economic opportunities, but also limit their spirits and dreams. Cultural dogma often confines girls to limited, undervalued lives within the confines of their homes. Yet, here in Tarun, we had the privilege of witnessing a profound, sweeping change, led by the extraordinary girls who defied generations of entrenched gender norms.

In 2015, when we began our journey in the Tarun block of Ayodhya (then Faizabad) district, we were acutely aware of the harsh realities. A significant number of families belonged to Scheduled Castes (SC) and Most Backward Castes (MBC), communities that lacked crucial knowledge about health, nutrition, and government services. Poverty was rampant, resulting in severe malnutrition, limited access to education, and a cycle of despair. Adolescent girls bore the brunt of these challenges. They faced violence in public spaces, were denied education, grappled with menstrual and reproductive issues, and endured severe anemia. Their dreams were stifled, and their potential lay dormant.

Our vision was clear: to empower adolescent girls, not just with education, health, and opportunities but also with confidence, self-belief, and the freedom to explore the world. The path we forged to facilitate change was intricate and required a multi-faceted approach. We were aware that our initiatives were likely to provoke backlash from the local communities, so we meticulously crafted strategies and fostered meaningful partnerships with the community, the village *panchayats*, government departments, expert professionals (consultants), and other organisations who supported our cause. Our approach was deliberate, taking one step at a time but working on multiple fronts.

On one front, we directly engaged with the girls, to broaden their horizons, and simultaneously, fostered connections with their families and local institutions. The initial hurdles were formidable. Girls hesitated to participate, parents were reluctant, and communities were skeptical. Nevertheless, we forged ahead.

To create safe spaces for the girls, PANI established resource centres (RCs) in each panchayat. The RCs were pivotal to our strategy, reaching all *gram panchayats*[1] in the areas. Each RC was responsible for fifty girls, grouped into two units of twenty-five each. These centres became havens for the girls to share, discuss, and support one another. Through discussion groups, study sessions, sports facilities, career counseling, and information resources, the RCs facilitated empowerment and transformation. Resource centre facilitators, chosen from among the girls, played a central role. We also recruited local staff, known as *didis* and *bhaiyas*, who became trusted mentors. With deep sensitivity, they engaged with each girl individually and at the same time also engaged with parents, fostering acceptance of new behaviours.

Despite initial resistance, the programme has reached over twenty-two thousand girls in eight years. Girls whose journeys are nothing short of remarkable. They have broken free from traditional constraints, excelling in sports, working in companies, joining the armed forces, pursuing careers in music, and securing higher education at prestigious universities. These young women's determination has left an indelible mark on their communities. Today, PANI operates an academy where girls receive training to serve as professionals at the grassroots level, either within PANI or elsewhere. This initiative enables us to extend the values of freedom and equality exponentially, further igniting the flames of empowerment.

---

1 *Gram panchayat, panchayat*: village council; a basic governing institution (political) in Indian villages, acting as the village's cabinet

As you turn the pages of this book, you will meet some of these girls who have conquered immense obstacles, transcending limitations that once seemed insurmountable. Their stories share a common thread—an unyielding spirit and an unwavering belief in their own agency. These stories bear witness to the untapped potential within every girl and serve as a powerful reminder that we all possess the capacity to challenge the status quo and shape our destinies.

My deepest gratitude goes to the girls who have shared their journeys and to the individuals and organisations that have supported PANI and its mission. The generous backing of our donors and the dedication of PANI's staff and consultants made this work possible. Rekha Saleela Nair, with her countless hours of engagement with the girls and their support team, has masterfully woven their experiences into words. Her work sheds light on the complex web of social norms that shaped these girls' lives and illuminates their transformative journey.

As we press onward in Uttar Pradesh our aspiration is that these stories become a wellspring of inspiration for all: the girls, the local communities, people across India, and the broader global community. May these narratives ignite a spark within you, prompting the questioning of entrenched norms, the embracing of your own agency, and a collective drive towards a world where every girl has the chance to flourish, prosper, and realise her limitless potential.

*Bharat Bhushan*
*Secretary, People's Action for National Integration (PANI)*

# The Writer's Journey

**A**dventure came calling early in 2023.

I received an unexpected invitation to travel and document the journeys of adolescent girls in the villages around Ayodhya. The opportunity excited me. It also unnerved me. I felt I was about to embark on a soul adventure that would bring together two topics I was passionate about: women's leadership and stories. However, the prospect of travelling through the patriarchal innards of Uttar Pradesh was daunting. Born and raised in a matrilineal community, I was used to strong women who were comfortable being their own people. I could not help but wonder how I would navigate the cultural differences and rigid social gender norms that I expected to encounter during my sojourn.

My first day in Ayodhya dismayed me. As I sat by the banks of the river Sarayu with a friend watching the sun set on the horizon, I was acutely aware of the paucity of women around me. The few who were out walked with bowed heads and veiled faces, their diminutive body language offering a sharp contrast to the stiff, unyielding demeanors of the men milling around us. Despite being bundled in *salwar kameez* suits,[2] we drew cold stares that seemed to aggressively question the temerity of two women who dared idle by the river at sunset whilst *langoti*-clad men[3] and boys splashed in the waters below. It made me worry about what lay ahead.

But the girls welcomed me with big smiles and demands for selfies. They overflowed with bonhomie as they narrated incidents that had infuriated their families yet sounded desperately downcast when the conversation turned to their poverty, the draconian controls imposed upon them in the name of honour, the social backlash, and more importantly, their struggles against their own conditioning. As the girls spoke with me, I would often observe their mothers fidgeting behind screened doors in their tiny mud and brick houses. At times, it was a grandmother's face that tightened imperceptibly as she crouched on the mud floor watching her granddaughter seated on the *charpai* meant for the menfolk.[4] Many of these mothers and grandmothers had never set foot in a school. Most had been married as children, disappearing into the flow of their marital homes before reaching womanhood. Held hostage by a disempowering gendercentric

---

2 *Salwar kameez*: a type of suit worn especially by South Asian women, with loose trousers [*salwar*] and a long shirt/tunic [*kameez*]
3 *Langoti*: loincloth; a narrow strip of cloth passed between the legs and fastened before and behind to a string around the waist, usually worn by men and boys
4 *Charpai*: a traditional, four-legged woven bed that is used for sitting or lying during the day and sleeping at night

script that limited a woman's identity and roles to marriage and childbearing, they struggled to understand their daughters who, even at age eighteen, still had no desire to be married, preferring to study, wear modern clothes, ride bicycles under the blazing sun, and dream of leaving the village to work. I felt the weight of their bewildered resistance. It made me choose my words with care, to highlight their daughters' youth and the possibilities that lay ahead rather than remind them of the urgent need to marry off their daughters.

The pathos of the intergenerational conflict often caught my heart. I could see that, in these villages, a mother's resistance to her daughter's aspirations stemmed not from a desire to hurt or harm, but from an inability to understand and fear. It often reminded me of a still lake whose calm water had been disrupted by a splash. Every time a girl made a choice to claim her life for herself, she disrupted the ordered way of life that her mothers and foremothers had known. Her choice often rippled out to lap away at the bedrock of tradition, first in her family, then in her neighbourhood, and eventually in the entire village. The splashes caused by one girl inevitably provoked a backlash. It also inspired other girls to make empowered choices of their own, causing more splashes and ripples until the tides changed.

The choice between maintaining peace by conforming to expected roles and behaviours and making a splash by being their own person is the everyday reality of millions of young women in India and across the world. The stories of these girls are our own stories and our daughters'. The people, places, and events may differ, but as women and girls, we are all living similar narratives. I hope these stories will offer you insights into the deep-rooted nuances of everyday gender disempowerment and that you will be able to see with new eyes what it takes for a young woman to go against the flow when she makes an empowered choice.

My heartfelt gratitude to my mother, R. N. Saleela, who made it possible for me to set forth on this adventure, to Shipra Deo, my companion on this journey, and my mentor, Jordan Goldrich, who helped me show up with an open mind and compassion. My thankfulness to the people of PANI who embraced me as their own, freely sharing their food, spaces, and stories with me, and to the wonderful people at the Greenleaf Book Group who have brought this book into your hands. Above all, I am grateful to the young women for meeting me with open arms. It is my prayer that I have done your journeys justice. Through these stories, may you inspire many to make a splash and ripple positive change in our world.

*Rekha Saleela Nair*

# 1

# *The Warrior in Camouflage*

*Being able to value herself as more than good marriage material has empowered
Vandana to become a warrior for her country and its young women.*

Vandana looks forward to her Sundays. It is her day off
at the Border Security Forces Training Centre, when
she can retrieve her cell phone and call her loved ones
back home in Kalyanpur Chhitauna. Several hundred miles
away, Anjali Pandey, who oversees PANI's centre in Kalyanpur

Chhitauna, among others in the area, looks forward to her weekly call with Vandana. The bond between the two women is undeniably familial. There are very few girls in eastern Uttar Pradesh who would dare dream of joining the national defense and security forces. Matters of war, peace, and safety—be it of family, community, or country—have been the dominion of men for generations. These issues continue to be fiercely held male bastions. Vandana is one among a miniscule 3 percent of women in the Border Security Forces. Her journey here has been arduous, and Anjali has been an integral part of it.

Vandana's father and mother, Ramkishor Verma and Pratima, were farmers who eked out a meagre living off their land. Despite their poverty, Ramkishor prioritised his daughters' education and managed to find money for school fees month after month. His determination perplexed the villagers who believed girls had to be married young. Girls needed to learn to be good wives and mothers, capable of silently choking down their needs and desires to fully care for their husbands, children, and in-laws. This was something girls could only learn at home, from their mothers, sisters, and grandmothers, and not at school.

The chattering in Kalyanpur Chhitauna crackled louder when Vandana and her sisters grew into adolescence. The villagers thought it was time Ramkishor abandoned his outlandish notions of educating his daughters and thought about their marriages. After all, he had five girls to marry off. Vandana was only in the eighth standard at school but as she heard the vehement opinions of the people around her and eagerly participated in the weddings of young girls in the village, she could not help but wonder what the point of her education was. Studies seemed futile when marriage and childbearing were her destiny.

Vandana was almost fourteen years old and in the tenth standard when PANI set up its resource centre in Kalyanpur Chhitauna. Ramkishor and Pratima were suspicious when Anjali came calling to invite the girls to an inaugural meeting at the centre and refused permission for their daughters to attend the meeting. Vandana and her sisters, however, were curious and snuck off without their parents' knowledge. Much to Vandana's dismay, the meeting proved to be a disaster. The girls of Kalyanpur Chhitauna had been sheltered all their lives and were raised to be fearful. Most of their decisions were made for them by their families, and they barely had the courage to form an opinion about what they liked and disliked. So when they were asked to sign up for the centre's programmes and activities, they were alarmed and refused, believing they were being inveigled into making a commitment that would get them in trouble.

Unperturbed by the hostile reception, Anjali continued to seek out the girls and visit their homes in the weeks that followed, determined to coax them back to the centre. Her persistent efforts intrigued Vandana, and as she interacted with Anjali, she came to know that Anjali was not only married but also had a young child. Vandana had never encountered a working mother before. The young wives and mothers of Kalyanpur

Chhitauna were seldom seen outside their houses. Slowly, a friendship started to bloom between the two women, and Vandana started visiting the centre, where she found herself captivated by conversations about the rights of girls. Despite her parents' restrictions, her visits to the centre increased, and she slowly started to push her boundaries.

Much to her mother Pratima's horror, Vandana slowly started to change. She took to wearing track pants and T-shirts at home; only to bed, at first, and then as her comfort increased, during the day as well. "I remember the first time I went to the village in my tracks," Vandana recalls wryly. "The ladies were so angry and complained bitterly to my mother. My mother was furious and often threatened to burn my clothes. I felt bad at times, but then, I would remember Anjali *didi*'s advice, that clothes are bad only when we are not happy or comfortable in them.[5] Didi used to tell me that I should give up wearing pants only if I did not like it, not to pacify the neighbours."

Vandana's obstinacy worried Pratima greatly. She worried about her daughter's future. *Who would marry a girl who dressed like a boy and was so outspoken?* Pratima would reprimand her daughter and try restricting her, but Vandana always managed to wheedle permission from her. Pratima knew she had to take a stand when Vandana started encouraging other girls in their

---

5  *Didi*: older sister; the proper noun or form of address for older sister, older female cousin, or an older woman, in Hindi and many other Indian languages

neighbourhood to join her on her visits to the centre, thereby raising the hackles of their mothers and other village women.

Besieged by angry demands to rein in her daughters, Pratima decided to ban Vandana from visiting the centre. It was a harsh blow for Vandana. The centre was a space where she felt seen and heard, where she could share her deepest thoughts, fears, and concerns, and even talk about taboo topics like her periods. She realised that her conversations and interactions with Anjali were shaping her into a better sister for the girls in her village.

Encouraging the girls in her neighbourhood to visit the centre was the least of Vandana's efforts to support the young women of Kalyanpur Chhitauna. She had even intervened in situations where families were planning the marriages of underaged girls and had managed to convince them to allow their daughters to study further. Vandana realised that the centre was the womb of her transformation into the warrior she truly was and knew she could not stay away. But Pratima remained deaf to her daughter's anguished pleas. It was only after Anjali had visited Ramkishor and Pratima several times that they allowed Vandana to resume her visits.

By the time Vandana was nearing seventeen, she had almost completed her intermediate schooling and was thinking about her future. Marriage was no longer a priority for her. She wanted to do more—graduate, work, and support her parents. Vandana observed that the women around her seldom sought help from the police, not even when they were in dire need. The marked absence of policewomen made the village women extremely reluctant to enter the *chowki*.[6] Vandana decided to join the police force, hoping the presence of a woman in khaki would encourage village women to use their services. It was a bold decision for a shy, naïve village girl. Like all other girls in Kalyanpur Chhitauna, Vandana was raised with warnings to stay away from boys. "We used to be terrified to step out of the house because of the boys loafing about in the village," she remembers. "We were told to stay out of their way so that we would not be harassed, nor would we have to endure their dirty comments. But when I interacted with *bhaiyas* from PANI, I realised that not all men and boys are bad.[7] This made me feel more comfortable with the idea of becoming a police officer."

However, Vandana's family was displeased with her decision. To become a police officer, she would have to qualify in the state-held competitive exams, which required coaching for her. The family's financial constraints made this an impossible dream. Vandana's sisters pointed out that no girl from their village had ever enrolled for coaching before and wondered how Vandana hoped to qualify when boys who had better learning opportunities had failed. Vandana remained resolute, refusing to be swayed by her family's doubts or the villagers' gossip.

---

6 *Chowki*: a basic unit of police presence in an area, usually a smaller police workstation, that is headed by a sub inspector

7 *Bhaiya, bhai*: older man; the proper noun or form of address for elder brother, elder cousin, or an older man in Hindi and many other Indian languages

As she entered the second year of her graduate programme, she decided to take on a teaching job to finance her competitive coaching. Those were not easy days for her. At eighteen, Vandana was juggling college classes, a teaching job, and coaching. She would leave home early in the morning and often return late in the evening. Impressed by her focus and grit, PANI decided to cover the costs of her coaching for a year. Vandana, however, did not qualify in the competitive exams the first time. The failure spurred her to try harder. She was determined to do what it took to crack the exams and become a police officer. Braving the displeasure of her family, she decided to move to Faizabad to seek better-quality coaching and the second time round, she aced the exams, qualifying not for the police but for the Border Security Forces.

Vandana's success sent tremors of shock and horror through Kalyanpur Chhitauna. The displeased villagers besieged her family with demands to dissuade her from joining, pointing out that the national defense and security forces were places for men, not young girls like Vandana. The vitriol of the village made Vandana question the wisdom of her choice. In desperation, she sought comfort from Anjali, who advised her to believe in herself and stay true to her dreams. The advice would prove to be invaluable, for when Vandana arrived at the training centre of India's Border Security Forces, she found herself truly alone for the first time in her life.

At first, she struggled with the rigorous training, but as the weeks passed, what once seemed impossible became easier. She started to feel more optimistic about her future with the forces. "Joining BSF made me realise that there is no truth in the belief that women are the weaker sex," she shares. "We may be lesser in numbers but there is practically no difference between the training that male and female recruits are put through." Vandana now thrives in her training programme and aspires to one day become an assistant commander or even an inspector general. To the world, she may be a young recruit in the Border Security Forces who dreams of greatness, but for the girls of Kalyanpur Chhitauna, Vandana is their warrior in camouflage who inspires them to bravely walk down untrodden paths.

# 2

# The Gully Girl

*Once labelled a disgrace, Riya's feisty spirit and cricketing wins
have made her a role model for the girls in her village.*

R iya had always dreamed of being a cricketer. It was an
unlikely dream for a young Muslim girl born to a village tailor in rural Uttar Pradesh. She was only eight
years old when she first joined her brothers in watching a
cricket match on television. Back then, television sets were a

rarity in her village. Every time the Indian men's cricket team played a match, the people of her village, Kakoli, would crowd into houses with television sets to watch and cheer India on. The charged environment in these houses and the frenzied excitement of the people enhanced young Riya's enjoyment of the game. However, it did not escape her that there were no telecasts of women's cricket matches, nor did anyone in Kakoli seem particularly interested in women playing cricket.

"Did women even play cricket?" she would wonder, causing her brothers to hoot with derisive laughter. "Cricket is a game for men," they would proclaim, scoffing at the idea of women and girls even stepping out of the house, let alone playing a man's sport. But their words did not deter Riya. By the time she turned twelve, Riya was pestering her brothers and cousins to let her play cricket with them in the *gullies* near their home.[8]

"I would plead with them to let me play," she reminisces wryly. "They would include me if they were a player short. Once my brothers realised that I could field well, they were more inclined to let me join them, especially when they were a player short. But they still would not let me bat. I would have to cry and fume to have a turn at batting." Riya's persistence paid off. She soon moved on from playing "gully cricket" and became a common sight at the village grounds where the boys gathered every day to play cricket.[9]

---

8  *Gully*: colloquial reference to the alleys and streets between houses where children play
9  *Gully cricket*: roughly translates to street cricket

At twelve, her passion for the game ran deep. It was not enough for her to merely play the game. She was determined to dress, walk, talk, and behave as a sportsperson would. She took to wearing track pants and T-shirts as her everyday attire, eschewing the voluminous salwar suits and veils that other girls her age wore. Before long, Riya's unconventional ways had riled the local Muslim community. The people in the village, particularly the women, complained bitterly to her mother about Riya's unorthodox behaviours and forward ways. Harassed by the complaints and taunts of the village women, Riya's mother would admonish, scold, and on occasion, beat her into submission, hoping that she would start to dress modestly in salwars, cover her head like a good Muslim girl, and stay indoors.

Fortunately for Riya, her father was a taciturn man who was the sole income earner for their large family of seven and was seldom home to lay down the law. She was careful not to draw attention to herself when her father was at home, ensuring that he had no reason to pay attention to her mother's complaints about her.

Riya's opportunity to pursue the game in earnest came in early 2016, when the team from PANI set up a resource centre in Kakoli. At the centre, she heard the bhaiyas and didis speak of the rights of girls, particularly to do the things they wanted to. Spotting her opportunity, she quickly approached Rajendra Tiwari, who managed the PANI centres in and around Kakoli, to muster his support for her game. Rajendra, who was a gentle, nurturing paternal figure, was immediately impressed by Riya's quick wit and assertiveness. He realised that she could play a key role in drawing the girls of Kakoli out of their homes to try their hand at games and sports. So he struck a deal with her. If Riya was able to co-opt other girls from the village to play cricket, he would buy them cricketing gear and equipment.

It was not an easy task. The girls of Kakoli were schooled to stay within the boundaries prescribed by tradition and convention. It was considered unseemly for an adolescent girl to be seen outside of her home, let alone run wild playing games as boys did. So when Riya went knocking at their doors, most of the girls refused to consider the idea of playing cricket. "The girls in my village would not listen," Riya recalls indignantly. "We are strictly told to dress modestly and stay indoors. The fact is, even if we were permitted to play, we didn't have the space. Most grounds in the village were taken over by boys for their games."

Despite the overwhelming reluctance, Riya managed to coax a few girls into joining her. Rajendra was impressed by her talent, grit, and leadership. "Riya is a little imp, but once she sets her heart on achieving something, she will make it happen," remarks Rajendra indulgently. "She was a driving force behind our efforts to popularise cricket and other games amongst the girls in Kakoli. While most of the girls struggled to understand the basics of the game, she was far ahead of them and was already playing well." By this time, Riya was determined to pursue cricket as a career. With Rajendra's gentle guidance, she soon found herself a part of PANI's under-19 girls cricket team and was able to play cricket to her heart's content every day. Once again, she shone on the field, and was soon selected to captain the team.

The change in Riya's cricketing fortunes gave her the courage and confidence to break further from the traditional mould and make bold changes. She was almost always spotted in a pair of track pants, a T-shirt, and a cap jauntily pulled over her forehead. Much to her mother's horror, Riya started to borrow her cousins' motorbikes to zip around the village and even got herself a fashionable buzz cut at the local men's salon.

"I saw my brothers and cousins come home with smart buzz cuts and wanted the same for myself," Riya recounts, with an impish smile. "I walked into the salon and asked them for one. The hairdresser did his best to dissuade me, going as far as to ask me to bring my mother. I brought in my mother for a bit to get him started, and then asked her to leave, so that I could have it cut exactly the way I wanted. Eventually, it was only when I threatened to go elsewhere that he gave me the haircut I wanted."

Rajendra remembers the furor Riya's escapade caused at home. "Riya's mother called me frantically because she had cut her hair short on the eve of a wedding. She had even razored her name on the sides of her head," he shares with a grin. "Her mother was beside herself. She wanted me to convince Riya to cover her hair and dress traditionally for the wedding so she did not disgrace the family."

Fortunately for Riya, the tides slowly started to turn. PANI's under-19 girls cricket team was winning matches at various sporting events at the block and state level. The wins made her family see her with new eyes. Slowly, her mother, siblings, and even the villagers started to accept her passion for the sport. Despite the disruptions to training caused by the pandemic, in 2022, PANI's under-19 girls cricket team won the second runners-up position at the 30th Junior UP Tennis Ball Cricket Association's Championship at Haridwar. This win and the media coverage it received proved to be a game changer for Riya. All at once, the attitudes in her family and village shifted. Riya's mother was proud of her achievements, more so when the people of Kakoli congratulated her on Riya's success and remarked how well she was doing as a cricketer. Her brothers, who once made her beg to be included in their games, now invited her to play under the pretext of checking how good her game was. Much to Riya's joy, her success inspired the girls in Kakoli to slowly emerge from their houses and participate in sports. It was a validation of the self-belief, courage, and tenacity she had demonstrated over the years to follow her dream. She was quick to encourage the girls who sought her out and silence any naysayers who attempted to dissuade them.

Riya now dreams big and explores new ways to live her life authentically. She plans to continue her education in the field of sports, looking ahead to the day when she is a professional player representing India internationally. She has come a long way from the gullies of Kakoli and refuses to turn back.

"I want to become a famous cricketer," she says determinedly. "I want the people in my village to watch me playing on the television and be reminded of all the times when they mocked, harassed, and looked down on a young girl whose dream was to play cricket. I am very brave, and I will achieve my dream. I won't let go."

# 3

## The Live Wire

*Kajal's passion for electrical work proves to people that there
is no such thing as boys' work and girls' work.*

Kajal is a live wire. As a young girl, she would constantly
fiddle with gadgets and enthusiastically volunteer for
any minor electrical or electronic repair work around
the house. Be it changing a light bulb or fixing small issues
with the television, Kajal was always the first to show up. "My

*dadaji* is the one who started this practice of calling me for electrical work," she says with a big grin.[10] "Even if I did not know how to do it, he would yell, 'Bring Kajal here, she can fix it!' I liked it very much. I didn't even mind the small electric shocks I got while repairing something."

Kajal's father, Kripa Shankar, was a humble farmer in Para Ram village. Despite his low income, Kripa Shankar was determined that his daughters and sons be educated so they were employable. Kajal was therefore encouraged to use her time to study rather than be swamped with household chores or work in the fields. Unlike most other girls in Para Ram, Kajal did not rush home from school to a horde of household chores but would often stay to play games like volleyball and *kabaddi*.[11] The freedom she enjoyed was unusual for a girl in Para Ram, and it gave her the space to dream big. She was inspired by her *chacha*, an army man, and decided that she would enlist when she grew up.[12]

However, theirs was still a traditional home built on hierarchy, where respect for elders was paramount and communication between generations was often stilted. Kajal did not have the freedom to speak freely and openly with her parents. Her older sister, who was her confidant, served as the conduit between

---

10 *Dadaji*: paternal grandfather; the proper noun or form of address for the paternal grandfather in Hindi and many other Indian languages

11 *Kabaddi*: a contact team sport of Indian origin played by teams of seven on a circular court, where players attempt to tag their opponents while repeating the word "kabaddi"

12 *Chacha*: uncle; a proper noun or form of address for a father's younger brothers, in Hindi and many other Indian languages

Kajal and her parents. "I usually talk to my sister, and then my sister speaks to my parents," she explains. "Even when it was time to pay my college fees, I would tell my sister and she would convey it to my parents."

Kajal was delighted when PANI opened its resource centre in Para Ram. She welcomed the opportunity to meet new people and learn new things. At first the centre was a space where Kajal could read books, play games, and participate in conversations about women's rights, equality, and empowerment. But when financial challenges threatened to disrupt her studies after tenth standard, Kajal was able to continue into intermediate school because of the financial aid from the centre. In time, the centre, with its didis and her friends from the village, became a safe space for her to share her feelings and thoughts openly. "I used to come to the centre and tell Didi everything that was on my mind, even things like periods, which I could not talk about at home," she shares. "It felt good to be able to talk freely."

In millions of households across India, menstruation is a ladies' problem and a taboo topic for conversation. The first menstrual cycle often marks the initiation of young girls into the shadowy, secretive world of myths, superstitions, and rules that surround their period. With minimal words and harsh scoldings, they are made keepers of a dirty secret that they are honour bound to hide from the world for most of their adult life. In Kajal's home too, the women seldom spoke of their periods. During that time of the month, the girls would unobtrusively retreat from their regular routine into a quiet corner of the house so they did not defile people, furniture, or things with their touch. Packets of sanitary napkins, carefully wrapped in old newspaper or black plastic covers, would be secreted into hidden niches in their rooms. Any discomfort was to be borne in stoic silence.

Kajal would often worry about her sister's pain, discomfort, and fatigue every time she had her period. Being unable to discuss it openly at home or with friends meant she had almost no opportunity to help her sister or understand menstruation in terms of her own physiological functioning. At the centre she was able to find answers to her questions about menstruation. Her worries were assuaged when she heard other girls talk about their period struggles, attended medical camps, spoke to doctors, and often got medicines for her sister.

When Kajal was designated as the block leader for Para Ram, she would make a list of the girls' problems, including menstruation challenges, and present them at the block leaders meetings with the PANI team. "At first, I did not feel comfortable talking to bhaiyas about periods. We had been taught to not talk about it in the presence of men," she shares candidly. "But soon all of us were speaking freely. Once I got confident speaking at meetings, I found myself becoming comfortable speaking at home as well."

Kajal's newfound confidence in talking about taboo topics like menstruation slowly brought about changes in her home as well. It became easier for her to co-opt her brothers and male cousins to help with household chores. She soon noticed the women in her family had dispensed with the plastic and newspaper camouflages and were carrying their sanitary napkins openly. "Things have changed in our house," she says with a grin. "I encourage my younger brothers to do household chores like sweeping by telling them that I will give them five rupees or that I will let them play with the phone. Now there are days when I ask my uncle and my older brothers to braid my hair when I am running late for school. In fact, the other day, my chacha helped me by buckling my sandals as I was leaving home."

Despite the changing familial environment, there was still resistance when Kajal decided to enroll in the electrician's course at a training institute in Faizabad. Kajal's parents were reluctant to let their daughter leave home for studies because of their concerns for her safety. More so because they worried that their neighbours would speak ill of her. Kajal's grandmother, on the other hand, was unhappy with her choice. She wanted Kajal to learn a skill that she felt was more suitable for women, like tailoring. "The people in the villages have very rigid notions of the kind of work women can do. So most girls opt for tailoring and beautician's courses because they are safe choices," explains Sima Verma, who leads PANI's programmes for the empowerment of adolescent girls. "We encourage our girls to break stereotypes by opting for courses like welding and electrician training. In fact, when we first approached training institutes to enroll girls in these courses, the principal and faculty were taken aback and hesitant."

Kajal was unable to understand her family's concerns about her enrolling in the electrician's course. In her eyes, she could do any job that the boys in the village did. Like them, she worked in the fields and even fought just as fiercely. When Kamlawati, who managed a cluster of PANI's centres in the region, stepped in to persuade Kajal's family, she discovered that a part of the family's resistance came from their financial challenges. The course would cost them three thousand rupees, which was a large sum for a poor farmer with a large family to fend for. Kamlawati was able to persuade them by pointing out that learning electrical skills would make Kajal employable and place her in a position to support the family once she got a job.

At present, Kajal is nearing completion of her three-month electrical basics course from the Leprosy Mission's Vocational Training Centre and has been attending interviews arranged by the placement cell of her institute. She hopes to find a well-paying job so that she can enroll for a bachelor's degree. She crackles like a live wire when she talks of her dreams and plans for her life. "I have many dreams and want to do a lot in life," she confesses, hope and determination writ across her face. "My dreams may seem disparate, but they are not. I will now start working, using my electrical skills and when I am eligible, I will try for the army also. I trust myself, my work, and that I will find my way."

# 4

## The Dholi's Daughter

*From being too scared to talk to her father to using her voice to build the life she wants for herself, Shivanshi today actively supports young women who are afraid to speak for themselves.*

Look into the heart of any Indian celebration and you will see a sweaty drummer or two thumping away frenziedly as they set the tempo for the people milling, marching, or dancing about them. Be it a festive *puja*, a wedding, a religious procession, or a ceremonial welcome, in India, it is the drummers' pulsing rhythms that calibrate the mood of an event.[13] But what happens when the lights dim, and the celebrations are done? In the villages of eastern Uttar Pradesh, a *dholi*,[14] the percussionist who plays the traditional *dhol*[15] drum, patiently waits in the shadows to be paid. No matter how gifted he is or how well he has played, he tends to return home with a pittance in his pocket and the pain of disdain in his heart. Vishun Kumar was one such dholi from Chitawan village, whose suppers were frequently laced with the bitterness of disrespect served in the aftermath of a celebration.

Vishun was a popular sight at weddings in and around Chitawan. But his earnings as a dhol player were inadequate, and he had to work as a daily wage-earning laborer to be able to support his family. Vishun had two daughters whom he wished to marry off as soon as they came of age. He and his wife, Malati, had been married as children, soon after they turned ten, and Vishun believed the sooner his daughters were married and settled in their husbands' homes, the easier it would be for him to breathe. So he worked hard to provide for his small family and was often away from home, leaving Malati with the responsibility of managing the house, raising their children, and caring for his aging mother. Vishun's oldest daughter, Shivanshi, was a shy,

---

13 *Puja*: ritualistic worship of gods; widely used in most major Indian languages to refer to the ritualistic worship performed daily at home, in temples, in offices, and in public spaces during festivals

14 *Dholi*: someone who plays the *dhol*

15 *Dhol*: a double-headed barrel drum that is widely used, with regional variations, in many parts of India

demure girl, who had little ambition for herself. Like most girls in Chitawan, Shivanshi went to school and in her spare time helped her mother with household chores. She thought herself lucky to be able to go to school. An early marriage had made school and education impossible for her mother. Shivanshi was grateful that her parents were willing to defer her marriage until she had completed intermediate schooling and turned eighteen.

Shivanshi was still in school when PANI set up their resource centre in Chitawan. The centre offered the girls in the village an opportunity to step out of their houses and escape the dreariness of their daily routine. At first, Shivanshi was nervous about socializing and would listen quietly to the conversations swirling around her at the centre. She came from a home where women were not encouraged to speak much or voice their opinions. In fact, Shivanshi and her sister barely spoke to their father. Her timid nature and painful shyness stood out, drawing the attention of Poonam, who was responsible for the centre's functioning. A nurturing woman, Poonam decided to encourage Shivanshi to emerge from her shell to voice her thoughts and opinions. As the two bonded, Shivanshi started to enjoy her visits to the centre and would look forward to them.

One day, while at the centre, Shivanshi was invited to sing at a talent assessment programme. Much to her delight, her singing was appreciated by the audience, with Poonam even suggesting that she consider pursuing it as a profession. The idea shocked Shivanshi. She had thought of herself as an ordinary, unremarkable girl, but the applause and admiration of the girls at the centre made her see herself with new eyes. For the first time in her life, Shivanshi thought of herself as special and capable of living an extraordinary life that no other girl in Chitawan had built for herself thus far. Impressed by her talent, and with Poonam championing her cause, the team at PANI decided to offer Shivanshi a scholarship to cover a year's tuition for training as a singer. But there was a catch to it. She had to move to Faizabad, which was a thirty-minute drive from her village.

It was a cause for celebration, but Shivanshi found herself quailing at the prospect of breaking the news to her family. The disdain her father endured for being a dhol player reminded her of the negative perceptions people had about entertainers, particularly women. Shivanshi worried about their reactions when she announced her intention of leaving home to train as a singer.

Her fears were not in vain. Both Vishun Kumar and Malati were astounded when she broached the subject at home. "What is this singing you want to do?" they demanded angrily of her. "Where will you go and sing? And who even said you can sing?" they asked, refusing to consider the idea. In sheer desperation, Shivanshi turned to Poonam for reassurance and guidance. Poonam astutely advised her to look for opportunities when her parents were in an amenable mood to present her case. Poonam herself took to visiting Malati in a bid to convince her. She knew Shivanshi's battle to secure permission from her father would be much easier if Malati was in her corner. So every time she spoke to Malati, Poonam made it a point to praise Shivanshi's talent and remark how lucky Malati was to have a gifted daughter. "I had so many conversations with Poonam," remembers Malati. "Each conversation helped me recognise Shivanshi's talent a little better. Slowly I started to realise that her singing abilities are a gift that not everyone has and thought, *If this matters so much to her, then maybe we should let her be a singer.*" It was thus that the family slowly started to come around to the idea of Shivanshi being a singer and moving to Faizabad for training.

When word got out in the village, people sniggered at Vishun Kumar. A man who was an entertainer was looked down on, but a woman who sang, danced, or played a musical instrument to entertain was objectified and regarded as being immoral. When the people of Chitawan heard of their dholi's daughter's dream of becoming a singer, they mocked him cruelly. "You play your dhol and your daughter will sing, dance, and do whatnot," they would say, winking at and nudging each other as they laughed pointedly at him. At times, they would include Malati in their ribald mockery, suggesting that she would dance while Shivanshi sang and Vishun played the dhol.

Stung by the possible loss of honour, Vishun rescinded his decision. Shivanshi pleaded in vain with her father to trust her, promising not to go astray, engage in immoral activities, or do anything that would shame her family. Malati, who was deeply angered by the villagers' risqué comments, was determined to support Shivanshi in becoming a singer. She, too, added her pleas to Shivanshi's, but Vishun Kumar remained deaf to them.

It was a tense time for Shivanshi, Malati, and Poonam. The date for Shivanshi's enrollment in the training programme had already passed, and her father showed no signs of relenting. Poonam recalls the uphill battle they had to fight. "Shivanshi's papa just would not listen to her or his wife. He was seldom at home, so it was difficult for us to meet with him as well," she recalls. "Eventually, it was Shivanshi's mother who proved to be our greatest ally. One morning, at seven o'clock, she messaged to let us know that he was home. We rushed over and were able to talk to him." After two months of persistent efforts, Vishun Kumar finally granted Shivanshi permission to move to Faizabad and train as a singer.

Shivanshi has been training to be a singer for almost a year now. She is also working, studying in a graduate programme, and has enrolled herself in a diploma programme in computer management. "I have never been happier with myself," she says with a beaming smile "I have transformed from a scared, shy girl who could not even speak to her own father into a woman who can speak for herself and handle life well. I found myself a job, a place to stay, and have a network of friends and well-wishers in the city. I did this through my effort and hard work. My life is good, and I know I am going to make a big impact in the future." Shivanshi is now a young woman on a mission, to use her voice to become a well-known singer, to build the life she wants, to help girls find their voices to speak for themselves, and to make her family proud. That will be the day the people of Chitawan will speak of their dholi and his daughter with pride and respect.

# 5

## Girls Can

Arati welds doors onto cars. She is one of seven women in a group of over two hundred men on the body shop floor of a leading Indian automobile manufacturer, and among two hundred and fifty women in a vast ocean of eight thousand men working at the company. Despite the overwhelming male population, Arati is quite at home. She wears the same uniform as the men do, works with the same machinery and tools, and even banters with them easily. When her male colleagues joke and ask her how she came to be a welder, she is quick to shoot back, "If you can, why not me?" Arati did not become a welder by accident. She chose to be one to carve a unique identity for herself and to prove a point to the people of her village, Takminganj. "People need to see girls doing the same work as boys," she explains nonchalantly. "If we are told we cannot do something because we are girls, then we must do it just to prove girls can."

But there was a time when she would not have dreamed of working, let alone as a welder. Born into a poor family in Takminganj, Arati was raised to believe that girls and boys were unequal and therefore had different social roles to fulfil. Her father, Ramsaran, was a farmer who supplemented his income by working as a laborer. Her mother, Vimla, managed household chores with Arati's help and worked in their fields. The family was desperately poor, and it weighed heavily on Arati. All through her childhood, she dreamed of being rich and dallied with the notion of working when she grew up. It was a dream because she lived with very little freedom. "The boys in the village would loiter about and harass us. It was a sport for them," she remembers wryly. "There was nothing we could do because we were constantly watched by the aunties in the village, who would gossip about us, carry the news home, and viciously ask our mothers, what kind of a girl have you raised?" Arati's four brothers kept a strict eye on her to ensure she did not behave in a way that dishonoured them. So, while she thought it unfair that the behaviour of the boys went unchecked, there was little she could do under her brothers' watchful eyes.

When PANI set up its resource centre near Takminganj, the villagers were immediately suspicious. They believed the centre posed a threat to the safety of the village girls—even thinking that girls were likely to be trafficked if they went there. So when Dharmendra Kumar, who managed a few of PANI's centres in the area, came calling at Arati's house, he was met with undisguised hostility. Ramsaran believed there was nothing to be gained by sending his daughter to the centre. Arati, on the other hand, found herself in a contemplative frame of mind. Her family's poverty and woes had worsened. One of her older brothers had married and moved out. Another had been abandoned by his wife and had to care for two young children. There seemed to be no way out of their situation. So when Dharmendra repeatedly visited with news and updates of empowering opportunities that the centre offered, Arati felt compelled to visit.

Her family was not happy with her interest in the centre and its activities. They planned to marry her off as soon as she completed her intermediate schooling and was keen that she focus on learning to be an exemplary homemaker. The centre was located quite a distance away, and Ramsaran was concerned that Arati's reputation in Takminganj would be tarnished if she was seen visiting. But Arati was unable to resist the promise of new opportunities and managed to convince her family to let her visit.

In no time, she became grist for the rumormongering mill. The village women were quick to warn her and Vimla that she was running the risk of being kidnapped and trafficked. They were incensed when Arati paid no heed to their dire warnings and maligned her even more. "It was not an easy journey for her," recalls Dharmendra, who had been aghast at the gossip. "People criticised her for setting a bad example and were so against her visits to the centre. It was Arati's burning desire to work and earn that propelled her forward." Her experiences with the villagers combined with the discussions she heard at the centre provoked Arati to question the social dictates and her own beliefs about what girls could and could not do. She found herself wondering why people believed employment to be the prerogative of boys only, when the girls of Takminganj were perennially working. "Every girl I know woke up early to finish their chores before they went to school. They would work again once they returned home," she asserts indignantly. "Even when there are examinations, a girl can study only after finishing her chores. The boys, however, roam about harassing the girls and fail examinations." The injustice enraged her, provoking her to decide that she would secure a well-paying job to prove to the villagers that girls were no less than boys.

Arati was now a girl with a mission. To drive her point home, she decided to study welding at a training centre in Faizabad. Her decision horrified her family. It was bad enough that she was thinking of working, but to know that she intended to do a man's job made it worse. Her parents refused to consider the idea. Their opinion was reinforced by Arati's brothers who furiously argued that their family's reputation would be besmirched. While there were concerns about her safety, the menfolk were afraid that they would lose face in the village if their household were to run on Arati's earnings. Arati tried pleading with her mother, but there was little Vimla could do against the resistance of five angry men. Dharmendra, who was a frequent visitor to Arati's home, tried to allay her father's and brothers' fears. His calm, stolid demeanor helped Ramsaran understand that Arati would be safe in Faizabad and have little opportunity to dishonour them. The family thus agreed reluctantly to let Arati leave home to study welding.

At first, Arati struggled with the demands of the course. She had not anticipated working with machinery and heavy tools or that she would have to learn allied skills like cutting and grinding. She questioned her choice when she found herself collapsing into bed, utterly exhausted, night after night after soothing her aching muscles and burning eyes with salves and medicines. It did not help that their trainers were skeptical and discouraging. "When a girl dropped out, some trainers would sarcastically ask us why we chose to study welding instead of tailoring or computer training," recalls Arati. "We used to tell them that if our own teachers break our confidence, then how can we succeed?" Fortunately, as the days passed, Arati became increasingly proficient at welding and, upon completion of her course, was invited to interview with one of the largest automotive companies in the country. The news incensed Arati's brothers, and a fresh storm erupted in their little brick house. This time, Arati stood firm. Her dreams were well within her grasp, and she was not backing down. With Dharmendra's support, she managed to convince Vimla to permit her to appear for the interview and was delighted when she was selected for the job.

Arati's new job was a godsend for the poverty-stricken family. Even though it meant a change in the family's fortunes, her brothers still resisted. They were worried about being mocked by the villagers for being maintained by their sister's earnings.

They also felt Arati would become too independent and uncontrollable. This time, Arati refused to beg or plead. She stood up to her brothers, pointing out that if they could work, then so could she. Her intention was to help her family as they did. Fortunately, she found an ally in Vimla, who, despite the opposition from her sons and the villagers, decided to let Arati take up the job.

Arati found her first day at work intimidating. The seemingly endless shop floors that buzzed with the sounds of huge machinery and working men unnerved her. But as she watched and learnt, she started to adapt and slowly started to enjoy her work. "People think women are physically weak and cannot do certain types of work. But skills matter more than gender," she pronounces confidently. "It is all about mindset and communications. For instance, if I am experiencing tiredness because of menstruation, I communicate this to my supervisor, who gives me a lighter workload for that day. It is a matter of believing in ourselves and knowing that we can find solutions."

Arati is finally on the path to building the life that she has always wanted for herself. The women of Takminganj still gossip, but their words fall flat before the enthusiasm of the village girls who are inspired by Arati. Change is in the air in Takminganj, and it will not be stopped by the naysayers anymore.

# 6

## Mirror, Mirror

*Sports have empowered Shivani to break free from the vicious grip of body negativity and low self-esteem to see herself with new eyes and pursue her dreams.*

Shivani is the apple of her parents' eyes. Her father, Ram Prakash, and her mother, Jasmata, are simple farmers who cultivate their land and supplement their income by working as agricultural laborers on crop farms in and around their village, Sarai Manodhar. Even though the family struggled to make ends meet, they were content.

Sarai Manodhar was a small village comprised of a little over four hundred families. The sex ratio and literacy rate here are higher than in many other villages across Uttar Pradesh. Still, the villagers continued to uphold traditional ways, particularly when it concerned the rights and freedoms of young girls. The women and girls of Sarai Manodhar were seldom spotted outside their homes. Shivani used to leave her house only to go to school, but unlike her friends in the neighbourhood, she did not come home to do chores or fieldwork. Her parents doted on her and encouraged her education. Despite their financial struggles and the conservative village environment, Ram Prakash and Jasmata did their best to fulfil their daughter's every wish. Shivani only had to express her desire to go out, and her parents would make it happen without a murmur, even though they knew the neighbours were likely to disapprove.

You would imagine that a girl so loved by her parents would be a happy, optimistic child. But Shivani struggled with a dark secret that tormented her day after day. She thought she was fat and could not bear to look at her curvy adolescent body. The mirror was her worst enemy. Every time she looked at one, she flinched. Her reflection made her feel unattractive and inadequate and filled her with unhappiness. Shivani longed to feel beautiful. She dreamed of wearing jeans and modern clothes like other girls, but instead, she felt compelled to hide her body in voluminous salwars to ward off critical looks and acid remarks from people.

The women of Sarai Manodhar were acutely aware of the power that beauty grants a young woman in cloistered communities like theirs. They therefore had definitive ideas about feminine beauty that they relentlessly impressed upon the young girls in the village. A girl whose skin was fresh and creamy like newly churned butter and whose figure was slender and graceful was deemed beautiful. They applauded the young girls who met or strived to meet their standards. The ones who did not were subject to merciless teasing, criticism, and even shaming. Shivani often endured jibes about her weight. *Moti*, they would call her over and over, sometimes in jest, often with the intent to shame.[16] She soon started to think of herself as less attractive, less smart, and less worthy than girls who were slimmer than her. Over time, her distorted body image eroded her self-esteem to the point where she believed she would never achieve anything worthwhile in life.

Shivani's self-esteem had ebbed to its lowest point at the time PANI opened its resource centre in Sarai Manodhar. The thought of a centre for young girls in a village where girls were not permitted to step out of their homes was intriguing. Despite her sense of hopelessness, and encouraged by her mother, Shivani decided to visit the centre. She was soon looking forward to her visits because of the opportunities she had to play games. It was the first time in her young life that she was playing games, and

16 *Moti*: an overweight woman or girl

she enjoyed it. "The village environment was not good, and so none of us went out to play," she shares with a grimace. "The centre was a place where we got together and did different things that we never had the opportunity to try before. We could talk frankly to each other, do activities together, and play. It was the first time I was playing, and I enjoyed it very much."

But change had only begun to rise and swirl in Shivani's world. While watching the youngsters play, Vikram Veer Singh, who ran PANI's competitive sports programmes, recognised Shivani's flair for kabaddi and encouraged her to try out for PANI's competitive sports programmes. Much to Shivani's shock, she found herself selected to be a part of the girls' kabaddi team. On the one hand, she was gratified to receive evidence of her worthiness, but at the same time, Shivani was concerned about having to cycle almost ten kilometers to Tarun to train with her team. She found herself wondering if she would be able to cycle the distance without falling or hurting herself. She thought she would be too tired to train after cycling to practice. More than anything else, Shivani worried about the sports attire she was instructed to wear for training. She had never had the courage to step out of her house in anything but salwars, and the prospect of being out in public in tracksuits and jerseys terrified her.

On the first day of training, Shivani left home in a salwar, deciding to change into her training gear at the grounds. It would be a tad easier for her to step out in her tracksuit into a field of similarly dressed girls, she reasoned. But it was not. The training attire clung to her body, revealing its shape to the world at large. Shivani was deeply embarrassed by her body and found herself unable to enter the field with her head held high. "I was so shy that I walked with my head lowered, refusing to look at anyone," she recalls with a gentle smile, her large black eyes shining with compassion for her younger self. "Sima didi of PANI understood my discomfort and reassured me. She told me that my embarrassment would fade as I got used to wearing my tracks and tees." Shivani's embarrassment did not escape her coach, Upendra Shukla, either. Understanding that her discomfort stemmed from a deeper, distorted relationship with her body, Upendra shrewdly advised her to focus more on building endurance and stamina than worrying about how she looked on the field or whether she would be able to keep up with the other players. Shivani followed his advice.

As she trained, she found herself becoming increasingly comfortable in the clothes she once thought she would never wear. More importantly, she started to feel better about her body. As Shivani's confidence grew, she found it easier to set out from home in her tracksuit for her daily training. She also found herself becoming increasingly assertive with the boys loitering on the village streets and corners who would try to harass her as she cycled out. "There are boys who mock us by calling us *kabaddi-walis* or ask us what we are learning at the centre," she explains, annoyance flashing through her eyes.[17] "Sometimes

17 *Kabaddi-wali*: a girl who plays kabaddi; sometimes used disrespectfully to put down women sports players

when I am cycling alone, they follow and try to stop me. But I tell them off so strongly that they don't dare come back," she says proudly.

Shivani soon emerged as a leader on the kabaddi field as well. In the aftermath of the pandemic, when the younger girls on the team struggled to regain form, Shivani was quick to encourage them as they trained. "The kabaddi team has girls in different age groups. Most of them come from very restrictive backgrounds," Upendra explains. "When we are training very young girls, we find that they respond better to a gentler, older sisterly presence. Shivani does an excellent job in understanding the temperaments and needs of the girls and helps them to do their best." Recognising Shivani's leadership, Upendra often elevates Shivani to the role of coach-manager and invites her to join him in leading the teams at state-level competitions. The opportunity to lead the team with her coach delights Shivani. More importantly, it makes her see herself with new eyes and dream bigger dreams for herself. "I want to become a good player and coach," she shares. "Wherever I go, I want to be known as someone who plays in the big leagues—at international events—and coaches well. I want to be on TV. I want to bring honour to my parents, my coach, and everyone who has supported me."

Shivani is twenty years old now and currently pursuing her bachelor's degree in physical education. She is already well-known in Sarai Manodhar and has begun to receive coaching offers as well as opportunities to organise and referee competitive games. She adroitly balances these opportunities with her studies and her training, keeping her eye firmly trained on her dreams. "I will become a well-known player and help many other girls like me learn kabaddi," she says with steely determination. "We girls should be courageous. No matter how bad we think our life is or how limited we think we are, we must believe that change can happen and strive to make it happen." These days, Shivani wakes up with enthusiasm and gratitude for her strong, agile body that helps her stride confidently towards her dreams and goals. The mirror has finally become her friend.

# 7

## From Fear to Freedom

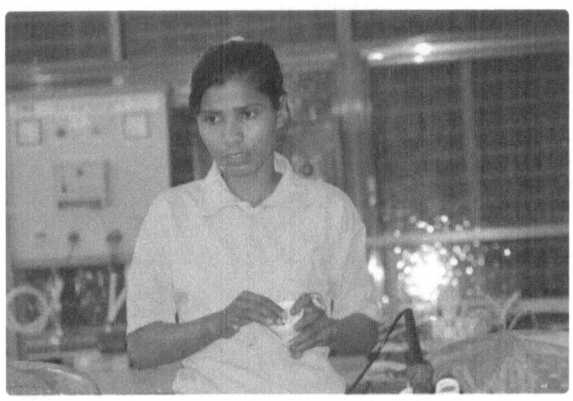

*Pooja's determination to provide for her parents wires her to break through tradition and learn a skill that is deemed to be a man's job.*

A t first glance, Pooja seems like a tough cookie. There is a no-nonsense air about her that tells you, no matter who you are, she will not suffer casual chitchat or frivolousness. Your smiles and efforts at small talk, be it about the blazing heat, the lush green sugarcane fields, or the bumpy, broken village roads, are likely to fall flat before her intense gaze. Her expression of perplexed enquiry will prompt you to get to your point so you can finish your business and be on your way to more companionable conversations. But as you sit back watching the tense twenty-two-year-old before you, perched gingerly on the edge of the seat, ruminating on her response, you have a moment of scintillating clarity. Beneath her guarded facade, Pooja is a fearful girl.

The insight may not surprise you. Fear is a trusted companion for young women and girls in villages across Uttar Pradesh. Right from childhood, through strict injunctions and directives first uttered in their caregivers' voices and then melded into their mind's machinations, fear stays the tongues of young girls, curdles their defiance, and torches dreams to ashes, ensuring that they remain reasonably safe in homes and communities where they are deemed lesser. Pooja has been dominated by fear all through her life, and she instinctively leans into it to navigate new situations, meet new people, and try new things.

Pooja spent much of her early childhood away from her family in Hathigo village. At first, she lived with her *nani*, her maternal grandmother, and, despite her tender years, helped nani manage her home.[18] She then moved across North India, to Ludhiana, and lived with her *bade papa*, her father's older

---

18 *Nani*: maternal grandmother; the proper noun or form of address for the maternal grandmother in Hindi and many other Indian languages

brother.[19] Her bade papa used to send her to school, and she studied up to the fourth standard in Ludhiana before returning to her parents and siblings. Pooja's father was a simple man who worked as a daily wage earner. He did not make much money, but he loved his children and wanted to give them the best he could. When Pooja returned home, she was duly enrolled in the local school. Hathigo was a small village of about four thousand people who were all known to each other. New entrants to the village were rare and the children of Hathigo were curious when Pooja suddenly joined them in the fifth standard. "No one knew me when I came back to the village," she recalls. "On my first day in school, everyone was curious and asked me whose daughter I was. I had to introduce myself using my papa's name. It was awkward, but I got through it."

Pooja soon fell into the rhythm of life in her family and village. She would bicycle to school with her sisters and the other girls every day. When school let out, she would hurry back home to help her mother with chores in the house and to work in their fields. As their primary breadwinner, Pooja's father would be out all day, taking on different jobs to earn money to meet his family's needs. It was therefore left to the womenfolk to cultivate the fields. Pooja and her sisters were determined to help their parents and worked hard on their

---

19 *Bade papa*: paternal uncle who is older than one's father; proper noun or form of address for the father's older brothers in Hindi and many other Indian languages

family's land. They sowed and harvested wheat, picked and cleaned *lobia* beans for their brothers to sell in the local market, and tended to the land.[20] The girls would return home late in the evening and cook for the family. Their hard work and grit won the admiration of the people of Hathigo, who would often ask her parents how they would manage once the girls were married off. However, despite their hard work, the family struggled to make ends meet, forcing Pooja to discontinue her studies after intermediate school. By then, her education had become a privilege the family could no longer afford.

Young girls dropping out of school was a common phenomenon in Hathigo. Only about half of the female population had a formal rudimentary education. Many of the villagers were either too poor to educate their daughters or would want to marry them off young. While many girls accepted their lot, Pooja was extremely disheartened when she had to drop out. Her family's poverty often made her think about seeking employment, but it was a thought she did not dare voice out loud for fear of offending her father or inviting his wrath. It was at this juncture Pooja discovered PANI's resource centre. The heavens, it seemed, had answered her prayers. For the first time in her life, she was among people who understood her burning desire to work rather than criticise or judge her for it.

Pooja's zeal impressed everyone at the centre, particularly Jameel Ahmad, who was responsible for the smooth

---

20 *Lobia beans*: black-eyed beans, black-eyed peas, cow peas

functioning of a cluster of centres in the region. Jameel was often in Hathigo for work and was a welcome guest in households across the village. For the girls, he was a kindly older brother who listened patiently to them and supported them in pursuing dreams that they were unable to voice to their families. Pooja found it a relief to talk to Jameel about her desire to mitigate her family's poverty. She was keen to enroll in a course in the skills development programme that PANI was facilitating through its partnership with the Leprosy Mission's Vocational Training Centre in Faizabad. When Pooja sought Jameel's advice, it occurred to him that she would make a good candidate for the electricians' course. For the people of Hathigo and in the surrounding villages, an electrician was always a man. Jameel and his colleagues at PANI were keen to challenge this stereotype and were looking for courageous young girls who would be willing to enroll in the electricians' course. Pooja, in Jameel's eyes, fit the bill. He decided to sound her out and was pleased when she responded with enthusiasm. "I liked the idea of doing the electricians' course," Pooja shares. "I thought if I can learn to do wiring and use electrical tools, then I can do something with this knowledge."

Emboldened by visions of a prosperous future, Pooja bravely decided to seek her father's blessings to travel to Faizabad for her studies. But her father was resistant and refused to grant her permission. The people of Hathigo, as in other parts of eastern Uttar Pradesh, believe it is a man's responsibility to provide for his womenfolk and protect them. His honour depends on it.

Pooja's father was willing to allow his daughter to work if her heart was set upon it. But the question weighing on his mind was how could he protect her when she lived away from home? Perhaps he also worried about the implications of her choice of career. When Pooja's explanations went unheeded by her parents, it fell to Jameel to persuade him. Jameel remembers his visit to Pooja's home. "I explained to *Chachaji* that his fear was stopping Pooja from going out to learn new skills and achieve things in life," he shares with a smile.[21] "I asked him to let her study in Faizabad because it is only when she leaves home that she will truly learn to do things for herself." Jameel was able to reassure Pooja's family and secure their blessings for her to study in Faizabad.

It was an exciting time for Pooja and a terrifying one too. The prospect of leaving home to move to a new place with new people and routines made her anxious. She realised that change and freedom were more attractive propositions in one's imagination. Neither were easy to embrace or adapt to in real life. Her early days at the training centre were a struggle for Pooja. All at once, the restrictions that confined her to the house were gone. She was bewildered by the array of new choices she needed to make as she navigated through her classes and her life in the hostel. She had the freedom to mingle with other girls and befriend them but was not sure

---

21 *Chachaji*: uncle; a proper noun or form of address for a father's younger brothers in Hindi and many other Indian languages

how to. She no longer had to rush back from school to complete chores or work in the fields. For the first time in her life, she could focus on her studies and only that. A new path was unfolding before her.

Despite her fears, she walks on courageously looking ahead to a brighter, better future for her and her family. "My dream is to earn money for my parents," she shares with a quiver. "Sometimes I worry whether I can achieve it. I am afraid but I tell myself to be brave and trust myself. After all, I have come so far. I will fulfil my dreams and my father's too." The mettle in her voice gives it away. Pooja may be a tough cookie, but it is not her demeanor that makes her so. It is her journey from fear to freedom, of eschewing traditions to forge her destiny through courageous choices, that makes her a force to reckon with.

# 8

## And Her Picture Changes

*Working as a chauffeur has granted Saloni the financial stability and self-confidence to rise above a traumatic past and live life with hope.*

A woman wracked by abuse is like a dramatic painting. At first, our eyes are drawn to the obvious, the swollen, bruised body, the breakages, and the wild, desperate eyes. Slowly, the subtler nuances begin to register. We see the hunted look, the muffled sobs, a body taut with terror, and the wary glances that scan faces and shadows in abject fear. This is what many of us see when we look upon a woman who has experienced abuse and violence. We seldom see the gaslighting and the games of control and manipulation that an abuser uses to orchestrate violence upon the body, mind, and spirit. These games are like the intricate patterns of the canvas that are enmeshed with the colors of the painting. One sees it and one does not. This is why the truth of a survivor's story can seem stranger than fiction, like nineteen-year-old Saloni, whose tumultuous journey makes a far more gripping story than any prime-time television soap opera that millions across India are addicted to.

Saloni was born in an impoverished family in Chakrasenpur village. Her father, Uday Raj, worked as a *mistri*, a construction foreman, and was the sole breadwinner for their family of eight.[22] Theirs was a miserable home. Every day, Saloni's older brothers would demand money from their parents, verbally abusing them until they acquiesced. As little Saloni cowered in the shadows, watching the harassment her parents endured, she slowly learnt to choke down her needs. It was evident to her that in her family, the needs of the ones who screamed and threatened would take precedence over everyone else's. The boys took what they wanted while the girls learnt to go without. Saloni's mother, Prema Devi, was a frail, ailing woman. Her poor health precluded her from managing the house or

---

22 *Mistri*: a foreman or supervisor of manual workers in India

working in the family's fields. She often left the management of both to her daughters. Saloni was still very young when her older sister went away to study. Overnight the responsibility of the house fell upon her tender shoulders. "I was so small that I did not even know how to make chai," she recalls. "Still, I would do as much as I could." Uday Raj would cook before he left for work each morning, leaving Saloni to take care of the household chores and her mother. Her brothers would spend their days loitering about the village, coming home only to eat and sleep.

Managing the house and caring for her mother made it impossible for Saloni to focus on her studies or attend school regularly. Her brothers' explosive temper tantrums, their abusive language and behaviours had begun to take an emotional toll on her. Things worsened as she grew into adolescence. By this time, she was singlehandedly managing the home with very little money. Her brothers had taken to drinking and brawling in the village. They were quick to abuse her for the smallest of reasons. Overlooking the fact that she was barely in her teens, Saloni's brothers would accuse her of immoral behaviour every time she stepped out of the house and would fling plates of food at her if they found it unappetizing. In sheer desperation, Uday Raj and Prema Devi decided to get their oldest son married, hoping that marital responsibilities would sober him. Perhaps they felt a daughter-in-law would ease some of Saloni's burdens. But this was not to be. Her new sister-in-law soon joined the ranks of Saloni's oppressors.

Saloni was in the eighth standard when Prema Devi passed away. The grief of her loss coupled with the desperation of their financial stress and the growing violence at home compelled her to drop out of school soon after. Those were desperate days for her. "I felt so alone," she recalls with a catch in her voice. "I was constantly walking on eggshells around my brothers. I remember I was once late returning from my aunt's house. My brother beat me black and blue with a thick rod. At other times they would starve me, not allowing me to eat the food that I had cooked." The constant fights unfolding in Saloni's home made their family the laughingstock of the neighbourhood. To make matters worse, Saloni's brothers had started to bring their drunk friends home while Saloni, her sister, and her father watched helplessly. The abusive environment took a toll on her sister's health. She too was soon confined to bed, making it necessary for Saloni to care for her as she once did her mother. It was in those desperate times that Saloni encountered PANI.

When PANI opened its resource centre in Chakrasenpur, Sudha Tiwari, who managed a cluster of centres in the region, visited Saloni and invited her to the centre. Sudha's calm demeanor and warm manner of speaking appealed to Saloni. Very few people in her life had shown her kindness, and she took to Sudha at once. The fear of her brothers' wrath made her stay away from the centre at first. But when she heard about PANI's plans for the empowerment of adolescent girls, she started to sneak visits to the centre. It seemed to her that the centre was a space where she would receive the support she had craved all her life. More importantly, she realised that with Sudha's support, she could find a way to work, earn, and live the good life that she had wanted for herself since childhood.

Saloni found herself confiding in Sudha and her colleagues and, with their encouragement, decided to resume her studies. Going back to school was an act of inordinate courage for Saloni. She felt bolder because of the continual support she was receiving from Sudha and her colleagues. However, the viselike grip of an abuser runs deep into the psyche of their prey and is almost impossible to shake off. Saloni used to be terrified of going to school because her brothers would follow her, threatening to abuse and even beat her in public. Eventually, fearing for her safety, she took to attending classes a few times in a month and would appear only for her examinations.

Saloni started to explore the possibility of working when she completed her intermediate schooling. Her brothers' violence was escalating fast. "I was completely at my brothers' mercy, and had no idea what they would do to me or even to whom they would marry me off to," she recalls. "I knew I had to help myself." Her plight caught the hearts of the entire team at PANI, including Sima Verma, who, as the senior project coordinator, was responsible for the effective functioning of PANI's various empowerment programmes for girls. Sima was deeply moved by Saloni's struggles and resolved to help her. "We were considering how we could help Saloni," Sima recalls. "We realised the government's Pink Express bus service for women could offer employment opportunities for girls who could drive. When we asked Saloni if she would be interested in learning to drive, she jumped at the opportunity eagerly."

Saloni's decision to learn to drive was bold and risky. Women drivers were an uncommon sight, and Saloni knew the villagers of Chakrasenpur would disapprove when they heard of her driving classes. Worse, she realised that they were likely to mock her family, provoking her brothers to cause her grievous harm. But she was desperate and determinedly pressed on. Uday Raj willingly gave Saloni permission to enroll in driving classes when she broached the topic at home. Her brothers, however, were furious and heaped abuse upon Saloni. Recognising that her very survival hinged upon her learning to drive, Saloni bravely stood her ground. She woke up earlier in the mornings to cook, clean, and ensure that her sister was comfortable before she left for classes and would return to her chores once she came back home. Her brothers were relentless in trying to intimidate her into giving up her driving lessons. "Saloni's driving lessons were held in Faizabad and Tarun," remembers Sudha. "Her brothers did their best to prevent her from going to Faizabad. In Tarun, they would follow her during her classes, abusing her and accusing her of immoral behaviour."

A new storm broke loose when Saloni completed her driving lessons. A friend, who had been supportive of Saloni through her troubles, confessed his romantic interest in her to her younger brother. When her older brothers found out, they furiously dragged Saloni out of the house and beat her mercilessly, blaming her for behaving like a wanton and for having a secret relationship. Despite her pleas of innocence, Saloni was locked up, starved, and repeatedly beaten. Things came to a head when her friend, with his family, arrived to explain to Saloni's brothers that while he was interested in her and wanted to marry her, there was no relationship between them. The intervention incensed her brothers, causing their violence to escalate to extreme levels. When it became evident to Saloni that her life was in danger, she decided to leave with her friend and, eventually, marry him.

Saloni is finally on the path to healing, peace, and happiness. She owns a Škoda and chauffeurs a school principal in Faizabad. "I believe if I work hard, money will flow in," she says. "My husband is a good man. I never imagined being married like this, but it happened. I did what I had to do to survive. One day I will build a house and bring my papa to live with me. Maybe my brothers will make peace with me. Who knows?" Her wistful voice trails off as she looks ahead to a peaceful, thriving future. The picture is finally changing.

# 9

## Blue Jeans

Reema always thought her father seemed burdened. But she could not muster the courage to talk to him about it. Theirs was a traditional home where the men ruled and the women abided by their decisions. Reema's father, Shripal Nishad, was a farmer in Hathigaon village who eked out a meagre living by selling the vegetables he grew on his farm. It was not easy for him to earn money from farming, and Shripal's family often struggled to make ends meet. The burden of being the sole breadwinner was heavy, but Shripal shouldered it alone, believing that as the head of the family, it was his responsibility to go out to work and earn the money needed to run their household. His wife, Usha, and his four daughters had to manage the home and lend a hand in the family's fields when needed. The conservative mindset of Reema's parents combined with the family's financial woes meant hardship and deprivation for her and her sisters.

Most young girls enjoy dressing up in fashionable clothes and hanging out with their friends. But Reema and her sisters were rarely permitted to leave their home or wear clothes they liked. On the rare occasions the family went out, Reema would enviously watch the girls around her wearing jeans and yearn for a pair of her own. But Usha refused to pay heed to her daughter's pleas or tears, insisting that Reema be modestly dressed in salwars every time she stepped out. "I kept asking Mummy to let me wear jeans, and she always refused," Reema remembers wistfully. "But I kept badgering her, and even cried, till she finally bought a pair for me." It was an empty victory. Reema got her jeans, but she still did not have the freedom to wear them as often as she liked or even style them the way she wanted to.

Like most mothers in the villages across eastern Uttar Pradesh, Usha worried about the harassment, abuse, and even violence that the village girls risked every time they stepped out of their houses. They knew that boys would be loitering in groups around the village, looking out for girls to stare at lasciviously, make aggressive sexual comments towards, and even follow, demanding attention. Usha knew that a girl needed to do nothing to draw their unwanted attention. She also knew that the villagers of Hathigaon would dismiss the harassment as the youthful antics of young boys but would direct their ire upon the hapless girls who were targeted by them. Unable to fight the system, Usha tried to protect Reema by refusing to allow her to wear her jeans outside the house unless she was fully and modestly covered up.

The family's financial struggles had intensified by the time Reema reached the tenth standard, and it seemed unlikely that she would be able to study beyond intermediate school. This was a blow for her. Reema had always enjoyed her studies and dreamed of becoming a science graduate one day. Now it seemed that her life, like her mother's, would be limited to the house. Reema's parents were skeptical when PANI opened a resource centre in the village and invited Reema to visit. They thought it was point-less for their daughters to be squandering their time at the centre when they could be working at home or in the fields. But when the team from PANI visited her home a few times to talk about the activities at the centre, Reema's interest was piqued, and she cajoled Usha into letting her go with the other girls.

Reema's visits to PANI's resource centre started to rekindle her dream of studying further. She found herself participating in conversations and discussions about women's rights that challenged her traditional notions about how women should dress, behave, and—more importantly—about the roles that women play in families. The discussions changed the way she viewed life. She started to think about the difference she could make to her family if she were to work and earn. She would not only be able to alleviate their family's financial difficulties but would also be able to educate her sisters and help them get jobs. She suddenly realised that she could choose to stand on her feet and live a life that she wanted for herself.

As she started to envision a better life for herself and her family, Reema also started to speak up about her desire to study.

"Reema's attitude changed dramatically once she started coming to the centre," remembers Jameel Ahmad, who managed a cluster of PANI resource centres around Hathigaon. "From a young girl who was resigned to living a life of poverty and drudgery, she saw new opportunities and became so determined to learn a skill that would make her employable that she would even tell her mother, "Give me two less *rotis* but let me study."[23]

When PANI ran a skill development camp at the resource centre, Reema found herself gravitating towards retail sales and thought it would be an interesting area for her to work in. She broached the idea of enrolling for the course at home, begging her mother to talk to her father about it. However, the proposition angered Shripal Nishad. "My house does not need to run on my daughter's earnings," he fumed, refusing to even consider the thought of letting Reema enroll in the retail sales course. This time Reema was not willing to give up on her dream. She persistently badgered her mother to coax her father into permitting her to study and work. Both Shripal and Usha were visited by team members from PANI who spoke to them about the opportunities that lay before Reema and the entire family if they permitted her to study and work. But her parents continued to be reluctant because of their concerns for Reema's safety. In their eyes, a girl who lives away from home has far too much freedom and therefore is vulnerable to harm. They argued that she could bring disgrace and disrepute to herself and her family because

---

23 *Rotis*: an Indian unleavened flatbread that is usually cooked over a griddle

she was beyond the control of her parents. "We tried telling them that Reema would be staying in a hostel that had strict rules governing the girls' movements and the visitors they could receive," recalls Jameel of his conversations with Shripal. "We even invited them to come to see the hostel and speak to the authorities there, so they could understand that Reema would be protected and safe. We persisted, and eventually they relented."

At twenty-one, Reema's dreams are finally coming to life. She works with the production unit of a private company in Bhiwandi, Haryana, and is building a better life for herself and her family, one that will free her from the drudgery of poverty. Her sisters aspire to be like her: to study and work. Reema is happy and optimistic about her life and her future, as well as about the changes that have unfolded in her family. "My parents have changed a lot," she shares with a happy laugh. "Nowadays, when I wear jeans, Mummy tells me that I look good."

# 10

## Last but Not Least

*Antima smiles as she can now see infinite possibilities in her future for her to serve and contribute to her country, community, and family.*

t is a rare Indian home that does not welcome a guest. Be it a dung-washed mud house in the village, a modest, small townhouse, or a modern apartment in a bustling city, guests are usually welcomed with warm smiles and open arms. They are ushered into the best, most comfortable seats in the house. Cool water is offered to slake their thirst, and then tea with an array of delicious refreshments is pressed upon them. But in the villages of eastern Uttar Pradesh, there is one guest who is often met with disappointed sighs, resigned silence, and sometimes even hostility: a newly born girl. Daughters in this part of India tend to be considered a liability. So much so that it was common for families with a daughter or two to name newborn girls Antima, which translates to "the last one," as a plea to the gods to henceforth bless them with boys only.

One such Antima lived in the village of Sihoriya. She was the third and the last girl in a brood of six children. Little Antima grew up hearing stories of brave leaders from India's independence movement. It made her yearn to serve her country, and by the time she turned eleven, Antima had decided to join the army when she grew up. Unfortunately, Antima lost her father when she was still a child. Her older brothers, Sandeep and Kuldeep, though young, became the heads of the family. The brothers had traditional bents of mind and were deeply influenced by the conservative views of the people in their village. A man's honour in Sihoriya was determined by the conduct of his womenfolk. Sandeep, Antima's oldest brother, was determined to safeguard the family's reputation and ruled the household with a heavy hand.

Antima was terrified of displeasing her brothers. She would carefully listen to their disparaging remarks about girls who wore jeans and take greater care to dress in modest salwar suits, particularly when she had to step out of the house. She would go to the local village school every morning, and upon returning, immerse herself in household chores. Occasionally, she would join her sisters in their fields. Her brothers did not permit her to meet or speak to friends outside of school, so fearing her brothers' wrath, Antima rarely lingered to chat with her friends after school or even in her courtyard. The girls of Sihoriya were frequently harassed by village boys who would loiter around, taking vicious pleasure in teasing and tormenting them at every opportunity. Antima knew she would be severely reprimanded if her brothers spotted her walking past the boys or happened to hear that she had been the unwilling target of their harassment. "It would be the boys' mistake, but I would get scolded," she recalls sorrowfully. "My brothers would be furious and ask me why I was showing my teeth to the boys. I used to be too afraid to say anything in my defense. My older brother takes care of the household and pays for my schooling. How could I speak up?"

When PANI opened their resource centre in Antima's village, Kamlawati, who managed the centres in and around Sihoriya, visited their home to seek permission for Antima to visit the centre. Won over by Kamlawati's gentle ways, Antima's mother, Rajpati Devi, granted her permission. For the first time in seventeen years, Antima had the opportunity to participate in conversations, games, and activities with other girls outside of school. It delighted her, and she looked forward to her visits. When Sandeep came to know of his sister's visits to the centre, he put a stop to it, claiming that girls who were given unnecessary freedoms would bring disrepute to their families. Antima tried explaining to her brothers that the centre had books, radio, and art materials that would enrich her learning and development, but she was quickly silenced by her recalcitrant brothers. "Bhaiya believed we would gain nothing by visiting the centre," Antima shares warily, as she remembers her conversations with her brother. "He used to say that he knew everything. Whenever we tried to explain or request permission to tell him something, he would order us to not teach him."

News soon reached Kamlawati, and when she heard that Antima was unable to visit the centre, she decided to meet Sandeep to explain that she and her team were only trying to safeguard the adolescent girls' interests. Perhaps it was her calm, gentle manner but for once, Sandeep listened and was intrigued. He decided to visit the centre so he could see for himself what the girls were up to. "When Sandeep Bhaiya came to the centre, he saw young girls trying to play cricket," Kamlawati recalls with a smile. "I requested him to help them, and he got so involved that he started coming back to help the children learn the game." Sandeep was deeply affected by the fun, laughter, and joy of the young girls as they tried to play according to his instructions. He found himself thinking of his younger sisters who were cloistered at home and started encouraging Antima to join the girls in playing cricket.

Antima was surprised by the change in her brother's attitude, but she decided to take the opportunity presented to her. Up until that time, she had neither followed cricket nor knew how to play the game. Her initial efforts at playing were tentative and clumsy. But as she started playing and watching cricket matches, her interest in the game grew. It soon became apparent to Antima and her friends that to truly play well, the girls needed a public space where they could play without being challenged or harassed. Together, they identified a vacant ground in the village and petitioned the *mukhiya* to have it cleaned and levelled for their games.[24]

Antima was delighted, and nervous, when she found herself selected to be a part of PANI's under-19 girls cricket team. To attend her daily training with the team, she would have to leave school early and cycle almost fifteen kilometers to reach Tarun in time for practice. Antima was not sure if Sandeep would permit her to skip classes or ride down to Tarun every day. But much to her surprise, Sandeep proved to be encouraging. Gone were the days when her brothers reprimanded her for stepping out of the house or made disparaging remarks about modern clothes. Now Antima was scolded if she missed cricket practice. When the villagers of Sihoriya made snide remarks about Antima's training attire, Sandeep declared to all and sundry that his sister was a sportsperson and, therefore, would dress like one. Antima was aware that the freedom she enjoyed was precious. It made her want to work hard and conduct herself in ways that honoured her family. "When I first started training, I made sure to communicate clearly, fully, and in a timely way

---

24 *Mukhiya*: village headman

to my brother," she recalls. "Soon, people started to tell Bhaiya that your sister is a good girl because she does not loiter about or misuse her freedom. Their praise mollified my brothers, who encouraged me even more."

Sandeep's pride in Antima skyrocketed when she was selected to be a part of the cricket team that participated in and clinched the second runners-up title at the 30th Junior UP Tennis Ball Cricket Association Tournament in Haridwar. "When Antima was to travel to Haridwar, Sandeep Bhaiya called to tell us that he had bought her a new suitcase with wheels just for the trip," remarks Kamlawati, who was moved by his pride in his sister's achievements. "He has changed so much since I first met him. It is not just Antima he supports now. He has permitted another of his sisters, Susheela, to enroll for a skills development course in Lucknow."

Antima plans to continue playing cricket as she completes her education. While she hopes to represent India internationally one day, her childhood dream of being in the army still burns bright within her. It is not an impossible dream as one might imagine. Antima's daily rides to and from Tarun, her cricketing practice under the blazing afternoon sun, and her team's wins at tournaments can pave an alternate path into the army if she chooses to take it. Army or cricket, her dream is to serve her country well and win accolades. Perhaps that will be the day when the people of Sihoriya will forsake their prayers for sons and begin welcoming newborn daughters with hope and joy.

# 11

## A Songbird's Joy

*Despite the disapproval of her father and uncles, Laxmi is determined*
*to make her mark as a singer and help her family understand that*
*music is a sacred art.*

A songbird is an extraordinary creature. These small, fragile birds perch on the branches of trees at the crack of dawn and enthrall us with their beautiful songs and rich complex symphonies. As we delight in their joyful singing, we seldom think of asking the bird, "Why do you sing?" We listen with a full heart, knowing they are born to sing. Much like the songbird, Laxmi Bharti also knew she was born to sing. She had not even turned ten when she realised singing made her happy—so happy that it made eminent sense to her young mind to become a singer when she grew up. Little did she know that the people in her village, Barav, looked down upon singing as being a pursuit for women of loose morals. Everyone who heard of her plans waved them aside as child's prattle. But the flippant dismissals did not deter Laxmi from announcing her plans to the world at large.

Laxmi was in the fifth standard when she told her teacher that she would one day become a singer. Intrigued by her solemnity, her teacher asked her to sing and was immediately captivated. She recommended to the principal that Laxmi be invited to sing at school events and functions. Soon Laxmi found herself being called on to sing a prayer, a welcome song, or even a filler at the school's events. It was then that she realised her dreams of becoming a singer might be realistic.

But the tides changed when she entered her teens. Much to her surprise, every time Laxmi spoke of her desire to become a singer, she found herself being told that it was an unsuitable profession. "All a singer does is sing one song after another," people would say. "Where is the scope for growth and success?" Their opinions perplexed her, but Laxmi realised that the passion she experienced while singing was something she had noticed in well-known singers, and she was determined not to give up.

When Laxmi changed schools in the eighth standard, she decided to be more assertive about owning her passion for singing. Rather than wait to be asked or worry about how well she could sing, she decided to bravely sing from her heart, without thinking about people's opinions or words. Her melody and passion soon marked her as a gifted girl. Laxmi's teachers would often visit her home and urge her mother, Neelam, to have her formally trained. But this was not well received.

Laxmi's father, Phoolprasad, worked outside their village, which meant he left Neelam with the responsibility of managing the home and children. Phoolprasad's prolonged absences meant Neelam was functioning almost as a single parent. She was alarmed by the seriousness accorded to Laxmi's singing ambitions by her teachers and would claim helplessness when urged to encourage Laxmi. "What can I do?" she would ask the teachers. "If Laxmi leaves home for music training, the neighbours and villagers will gossip about her, claiming that she is headstrong, wild, and immoral. Besides, she is so young and will not be able to take care of herself if she goes away from home." Then, after silencing Laxmi's champions, Neelam would turn her attention to her daughter and scold her bitterly, urging her to take her cues from her sister and learn a useful skill like tailoring. Laxmi, however, was undeterred.

Laxmi found a new vista of hope when PANI opened their resource centre in Barav. When she found other girls at the centre taking up sports and enrolling for skills development courses, Laxmi was excited and sought help from the team to train as a singer. But opportunity came knocking before her didis at the centre could formulate a plan. One afternoon, as Laxmi was cooking a meal for her family, a neighbour dropped in with the news that a reputable music school was conducting auditions in the nearby town of Tarun. Laxmi dropped her ladle without a second thought, grabbed her cycle, and pedalled as fast as she could to the audition. A few days later, she learnt of her selection for music training. The break she had been looking for had finally materialised. But there was a catch to it. She had to travel to Faizabad every day for her lessons and training.

The news was not received well by her family. Terrified of the vicious gossip, both Neelam and Phoolprasad flatly refused to grant permission. Neelam's brothers, who were constantly at hand, also voiced their displeasure. Even Laxmi's younger brother was quick to voice derogatory comments about singing and singers. It seemed that everyone was determined to thwart her. Despite Laxmi's promises to behave well, the family demanded that she sacrifice her dreams to focus on a profession that was more appropriate for a girl. In sheer desperation, Laxmi turned to her didis and bhaiyas at PANI for emotional support and intervention. She pestered her mother to come to Tarun to meet Sima Varma who led PANI's different programmes aimed at the empowerment of adolescent girls. Sima was able to assuage Neelam's concerns and persuade her into accompanying Laxmi to Faizabad to explore the opportunity at hand. It was with great expectations that Laxmi took her mother to the music school. Unfortunately, during their visit, Neelam happened to observe boys and girls practicing their music in a single space. The realisation that the school was coeducational resurrected all of Neelam's misgivings about letting Laxmi live in Faizabad. Mother and daughter returned home without enrolling Laxmi in music school.

The menfolk in the family—her father, uncles, and her brother—were now extremely determined that Laxmi was not to be allowed to train as a singer. It left her no option but to once more turn to PANI for an intervention. This time, it was Udai Tiwari from PANI who visited the family. "I explained to Laxmi's father that the world has changed and continues to change," Udai reveals. "I clarified that it is only the school that is coeducational, not the living accommodations. Laxmi would have to live in the girls' hostel and abide by its strict rules." Despite the interventions and exhortations, Neelam and Phoolprasad finally allowed Laxmi to study music on the condition that she would commute to Faizabad and back every day. Laxmi knew it would be arduous but she was willing to bear any amount of hardship to be able to learn music. However, there are times when the body refuses to follow the mind. A few months after school started, Laxmi realised that the daily commute was taking a heavy toll on her. She was tired and unable to manage her studies, music training, and her chores about the house. More importantly, the constant demands and disturbances from the household made it impossible for her to practice her singing with the discipline, reverence, and effort it required. She was forced to approach her parents once more to seek permission to move to Faizabad.

Neelam, who had been observing her daughter's fatigue with concern, was now more amenable to Laxmi's request. She agreed to accompany Laxmi to Faizabad to identify safe, suitable accommodations so she could move closer to her school. But she returned home to face the wrath of her husband and brothers for what they thought was her irresponsibility. Laxmi too came in for her share of criticism and scoldings. She tried explaining that she was training to be a classical singer, learning *raag*,[25] *raaginiyan*,[26] and singing sacred *bhajans*,[27] but her words fell on deaf ears. Her uncles persisted in stating that she was learning titillating "item numbers"[28] and Bollywood[29] music that had overt sexual undertones to it. "My papa and uncles still don't understand that I am gaining an education in music," Laxmi states wearily, sadness stamped over her face and words. "Every time my uncle calls, he does not even ask me how I am doing. He only reprimands me. Despite my repeated requests, none of them have come to my school or talked to my teachers.

---

25 *Raag*: a piece of Indian classical music based on a traditional scale or pattern of notes

26 *Raaginiyan*: a piece of Indian classical music based on a traditional scale or pattern of notes

27 *Bhajans*: any devotional song in any language that has a religious theme or spiritual ideas and is sung at temples and spiritual gatherings

28 Item numbers: a musical performance that is often inserted into an Indian movie to entertain or increase its market value. It usually is catchy and tends to come with a sensual dance sequence.

29 Bollywood: the Indian popular film industry, based in Mumbai

If they did, then maybe they would understand. How can I help people who do not wish to understand?"

Laxmi's dedication to her art is absolute. She has enrolled for her bachelor's degree in music, which she plans to complete in parallel with her training. Her dream is to complete her education, secure a job teaching music, and to be known as a good singer. Hopefully one day, the men in her family will feel the joy in the songbird's music and listen without asking her why.

# 12

## Finding Her Feet

*As Shanti tailors new dreams for herself and her family, she challenges the deep-rooted beliefs people hold about the capabilities of and possibilities for young women with disabilities.*

Shanti's birth was not a joyous event. In fact, her arrival was met with deeper disappointment and dismay than the birth of a girl usually evoked in the village of Imiliya. It was not her gender that made her family despair. Shanti was born with a congenital limb defect that she and her family struggle to name to this day. If you ask her about her disabled leg, she will tell you that she was born with it because her mother, Indrawati, while pregnant, inadvertently stepped out of the house during an eclipse. Her conviction may startle you. But Shanti is not alone in believing her locomotor disability to be a retribution from the gods. Superstitions abound and govern everyday life in small villages with low literacy levels.

There were many in Imiliya who shared Shanti's belief and squarely placed the blame for her disability on Indrawati. Perhaps it was guilt, but Indrawati would often look at her baby daughter and wish her dead. She was painfully aware that a girl born with a disability in a poor home is disadvantaged many times over. Indrawati was racked with worries about Shanti: *How would she live her daily life? Would she be a burden on them? Who would marry her?* Indrawati knew that as Shanti grew up, her disability would make her an easy target for ridicule, gossip, bullying, harassment, and even abuse. No amount of consolation from her family or the villagers could change her mind that Shanti was better dead than alive.

Shanti's father, Channgulal, was nonplussed by his daughter's disability. But rather than wish her dead or hide her away, he was willing to seek medical help. As Shanti grew older, Channgulal consulted the doctors in and around Imiliya. Unfortunately, none of them were able to help him understand why his daughter was born with a disabled foot or suggest how to treat it. Channgulal was a poor farmer who struggled to provide for his family of six. Travelling to the city to seek expert medical advice was an impossible dream for him, and so Shanti grew up learning to navigate life with one able foot. Despite her limited mobility, she was allowed to go to school and managed to complete her intermediate schooling. But when Shanti's older sister was married off, the family's financial situation became even more precarious, forcing both Shanti and her brother to drop out of school.

Shanti's brother started work as a barber, supplementing his earnings by occasionally picking up odd jobs in the village. He, too, was married soon after his older sister. Unfortunately for Shanti and her parents, her brother and his new bride were reluctant to live in a joint family house with them. Determined to set up an independent house, they forced Channgulal's hand by refusing to contribute to the family's income and upkeep. To make matters worse, they were constantly at loggerheads with Shanti's older sister.

Those were difficult days for Shanti. Disagreements, fights, and estrangements over small issues were commonplace in their home. The grief and pain that punctuate Shanti's words whenever she speaks of her family is palpable. "There was, still is, no peace at home," she says sadly. "My *bhabhi* keeps saying unpleasant things to us.[30] My older sister and brother fight because my sister feels he does not communicate enough with

---

30 *Bhabhi*: sister-in-law; the proper noun or form of address for an older sister-in-law in Hindi and many other Indian languages

her. But we are poor and must share phones. It's not easy for us to call at will." Despite the everyday hostilities, Channgulal refused to let the disgruntled couple leave the family for fear of losing face. In India, and particularly in states like Uttar Pradesh, tradition places the responsibility of protecting, serving, and caring for parents and sisters upon the shoulders of sons. Channgulal was aware that his family would be severely ridiculed in the village if he permitted his only son to set up a separate house in Imiliya. However, the continual conflict between the family members not only exacerbated their financial difficulties but also made Shanti's family the butt of the villagers' jokes.

The sheer poverty of the family compelled Channgulal to ask Shanti if she would consider working and contributing to the family income. His request surprised her. The girls and womenfolk of Imiliya had little freedom and were seldom seen outside their homes. The only work they did was in and around their houses and farms. It was unthinkable for a young girl to be out in the village seeking employment. But Shanti was unwilling to disappoint her father and started to wonder what kind of work she could possibly do despite her disability. She realised that she was nimble with the needle and enjoyed sewing. In fact, her only source of joy in an otherwise dreary home life was sewing and embroidery, which she had learnt from her older sister. Therefore, it was only natural for her to consider work that involved tailoring skills. She decided to enroll in a tailoring course in Imiliya but was unable to complete the programme.

Shanthi's break came in 2016, when she learnt of PANI's resource centre from the girls in her village. Through them, she had the opportunity to visit the centre, attend meetings, participate in discussions about skills training for employability, and explore the possibility of taking a tailoring course that would help her find a job. When Shanti saw other girls at the centre enroll in skills development programmes and secure jobs, she felt encouraged to put her name forward as well. She was aware that her limited mobility and inability to remain standing for long periods of time would severely limit her options. Unlike most other girls at the centre, she would not be able to enroll in welding or electrical courses. After much discussion, the team at PANI suggested that Shanti study tailoring at the Leprosy Mission's Vocational Training Centre, which would offer her placement support once she completed her studies.

The idea excited and terrified Shanti. On the one hand, she wanted to learn a skill that she knew she enjoyed, get a job, and support her family. But on the other hand, the prospect of leaving Imiliya had never crossed her mind. She was aware that her locomotor disability made her more vulnerable than the average girl in the village and was apprehensive of the malicious gossip that would inevitably rise if she were to leave. Shanti's concerns were not unfounded. Even Channgulal and Indrawati were aghast at the idea of their daughter leaving home. They were concerned about her safety and worried that she would not be able to manage by herself. What terrified them even more was the reputation Shanti would acquire in Imiliya if she left. In the eyes of the villagers, there were no respectable choices of work open to a girl with a disability. Channgulal worried that the villagers would label him an irresponsible father, or worse, for living off his daughter's earnings. It was only after repeated interventions and counseling from PANI's team members that Channgulal agreed to let Shanti study tailoring.

Shanti's decision to leave Imiliya was an act of love and inordinate courage. "I left home to study a skill that will help me earn a living," she says in a downcast voice. "But in my village, people gossip about me. Since I have a physical disability, they say I am here to earn through immoral activities. I want to get a job, earn well, and live well, just to prove them wrong." Shanti has been working diligently at mastering her craft, hoping that her dedication and perseverance will help her get a good job with a company once her course is over. Her disability causes her great physical discomfort. But she is determined to get ahead and make things better for her family. Above all, she wants to show the people of Imiliya that while she may not have a physical foot to stand on, she can still find her feet in the world and achieve great things.

# 13

# Breaching Invisible Barriers

Twenty-one-year-old Nisha had always dreamed of working and earning her own money. As the eldest in an impoverished family in the village of Baisu Pali, Nisha had been privy to her parents' financial struggles from a very young age. Her parents, Ramnath and Ramawathi, were daily wage-earning laborers who barely managed to run their household with their meagre earnings. Growing up, Nisha was not allowed much freedom. She lived in a village that was dominated by people of higher castes who were overtly and covertly hostile towards families of lower castes such as hers. Caste is a heavy word in India. In villages across the country, it is your caste that determines how you fit into the social hierarchy, the privileges you may enjoy, and the power you can wield. The lines that separate the people with whom you can break bread and walk with, from those with whom you cannot are often invisible, but they work. Jameel Ahmad, who oversees a cluster of PANI's centres in villages around Ayodhya, is often privy to the different ways caste dynamics unfold in a small village. "There still are people whose thinking has not progressed with the times," he remarks. "They believe the superiority of their caste entitles them to demand service from people they perceive as belonging to lower castes, even if it violates their basic human rights."

The people of Baisu Pali constantly undermined and demeaned Ramnath and his family members. Nisha and her sister were continually reminded that they would not be able to achieve anything worthwhile in life because their parents and grandparents had not been able to achieve much. The unkind attitudes and harsh words made Nisha's parents worry about her safety. They were acutely aware that young girls belonging to lower castes occupied the bottom end of the social and patriarchal hierarchies and were particularly vulnerable to both caste and gender discrimination. "The environment around us is not good, nor are the ways of the people," Ramnath often said, restricting Nisha and her sister from stepping out of the house or dressing and behaving in ways that drew attention to themselves. While there were girls from upper caste families in Baisu Pali who studied in Faizabad and enjoyed some freedom to move around, Ramnath insisted that his daughters study in the village school and college, and only when they were accompanied by girls from families he knew well. His word was law. Ramawathi deferred to her husband's decisions in the running of their family and how they lived their lives. Every time Nisha spoke of finding a job once she completed her studies, her father would brush it off saying that it was not her responsibility to earn and support the family. In his eyes, Nisha was to study hard and marry a suitable boy her family chose for her.

Nisha longed for the freedom that most girls in her village enjoyed. However, the hostile looks and harsh derogatory words of the people terrified her into remaining within the safe confines of her home. The social environment took a toll on her self-esteem and confidence, making her dream of employment seem impossible. "I never ever thought it would be possible for me to leave my village, live in a city, work in a big company, and send money home to my parents," she says every time she thinks of her early years in the village.

By the time Nisha graduated, PANI had opened a resource centre in Baisu Pali. The young girls in the village slowly started to flock to the centre every day, where they had the opportunity to participate in conversations about gender, equality, and the rights of women and girls to live their lives as they wished. Nisha suddenly found herself in a safe space where she could brush the cobwebs off her secretly held dreams and explore new ways to actualise them. She found herself enjoying her experiences at the centre. Jameel and his colleagues at the resource centre encouraged Nisha to envision an empowered life for herself.

When they heard of her ardent desire to work and alleviate her family's poverty, they decided to help her identify skills development courses that would make her employable and support her in finding a job that would enable her to be independent. "After I started coming to the centre, I started to think, if the other girls in the village can go out, work, and do things for themselves, then I can do it too," Nisha shares. "I suddenly felt more confident about it."

Emboldened by the support she was receiving, Nisha decided to talk to her father about enrolling in a residential programme for skills development in Gorakhpur. Ramnath was at first enraged at his daughter's audacity. Gorakhpur was barely a three-hour drive from their village, and yet he was angered that his daughter dared think of leaving her home to go study. At the heart of his anger lay fear. He worried that the opportunity his daughter was so excited about would cause her harm and lead her to her downfall. Many girls from higher caste families in Baisu Pali were studying at the training centre that Nisha wished to study at. He worried about their reactions to Nisha's presence amidst them, studying, eating, walking, and breaching the invisible lines that separated them. What if she was kidnapped and sold off? What if something untoward happened to her? In his eyes, she was vulnerable, and any harm done to her body would dishonour him and his family. "There is no reason for you to work when I am here to take care of this family," he would fume when she tried to convince him over and over.

In sheer desperation, Nisha finally turned to Jameel for support. "I spoke to Ramnath Chacha about how the world has changed and that it is safe for young girls to go out to study and work," Jameel recalls. "Her parents were deeply concerned because they worried about Nisha's safety. We eventually were able to convince them that we are all at hand and would ensure Nisha's well-being." Eventually, Ramnath relented and permitted Nisha to enroll in the programme. It proved to be a game changer for her and for many families in the village whose daughters were already studying at the institute. Nisha was met with suspicion and hostility at first. It was difficult for the girls to shake off centuries of ingrained, caste-based beliefs and prejudices. Nisha too had to struggle with her own beliefs and fears. But as the days passed, the students had no choice but to abide by the institute's rules for equality and check their biases and prejudices. As the attitudes and behaviours of the students started to change, Nisha found herself increasingly able to dedicate herself to her studies. Her diligence as well as qualitative training and mentoring eventually saw her placed with a private company in Haryana.

Today, Nisha lives life with greater freedom and confidence. She dresses as she wishes, travels at her will, manages her finances and her life, and works at a job she enjoys. "When we do something for the first time, it will be daunting for a few days," she confides. "It is normal to feel afraid at such times. But if we take brave steps, it will become familiar and comfortable. More importantly, as we change, the people around us will also change." The people of Baisu Pali are friendlier towards her now. Nisha knows the invisible lines will not be easily erased from their minds and hearts, but she is confident in her ability to navigate them in ways that are empowering for her and others like her.

# 14

## Confidently Her

*Ekta's passion, confidence, and success at sports shatters villagers'
misconceptions about sports diminishing a girl's health, looks, and prospects.*

Ekta's calloused soles push back the hard earth as she leans
forward to regard her opponents. Beads of sweat dribble
down her face, but she is far too intent on the girls before
her to notice. Her long hair pulled back in a tight braid could be
a distraction. Swinging free, it is a liability on the kabaddi field

where her opponents can grab at it to bring her down. Ekta is careful to keep her hair out of their reach as she nimbly lunges forward to tag a girl before racing back to the safety of her team. Unfortunately, she is brought down by her opponents before she reaches home base. As Ekta disentangles and extricates herself from the pile of bodies on the ground, her disappointed eyes seek out her coach, silently asking for feedback. Her refusal to pause after a hard fall leaves a casual bystander in no doubt about how seriously Ekta takes her game.

Eighteen-year-old Ekta firmly believes she is inordinately lucky to have secured a place on PANI's kabaddi team. There was a time when young girls living in and around Tarun were not permitted to play games or sports, let alone pursue it competitively. Ekta was, in fact, the only girl from her village, Yadav Pur, to participate in the qualifiers held by PANI. She was able to because of her grandfather's support.

Ekta was born into a large joint family engaged in farming in Yadav Pur. Her father, Ram Manohar, worked in the family fields with the other menfolk. Ekta's *dadu*, her paternal grandfather, was the patriarch of the family and his word was law.[31] However, the inner apartments of the house, where the women and girls spent most of their time, was the fiefdom of her *dadi*, her grandmother.[32] So, while Ekta was close to her dadu, she

---

31 *Dadu*: paternal grandfather; an affectionate variant of *daada*, which is the proper noun or form of address for the paternal grandfather in Hindi and many other Indian languages
32 *Dadi*: paternal grandmother; the proper noun or form of address for the paternal grandmother in Hindi and many other Indian languages

still had to lead a sheltered life as dictated by her dadi. Ekta was permitted to go to school, but upon returning, she had to join her mother, aunts, and cousins to do the chores around the house and farm. Ekta's dadi believed that young girls were to be moulded and trained to be good wives and mothers. Dadi had been married young and had, in turn, married off her sons in their teens to pliable young girls who had adapted to the ways of the family silently and seamlessly. Ekta's mother, Lalmati, had arrived as a young bride in the family at the tender age of fourteen. In Dadi's eyes, Ekta and her sisters had to be married as soon as the family found them suitable boys and good homes.

This sheltered upbringing made Ekta a timid child. She did not like being a shy girl and yearned to be a confident person. To her child eyes, the police officers she saw around Yadav Pur appeared strong and confident. She imagined herself in a police uniform, walking about boldly as one of them, and decided that she would join the police force when she grew up.

The only time Ekta felt strong and confident was when she was running. Experiencing the power of her muscles and the sound of her feet drumming on the earth made her feel invincible. Eager to run, Ekta would participate in all the races her school organised. But they were few and far between, often leaving her longing for more.

Ekta felt she was being tossed a lifeline when PANI opened its resource centre for the adolescent girls of Yadav Pur. With her dadu's permission, and much against her grandmother's wishes, Ekta started to visit the centre frequently, lured by the opportunity to play games. "PANI came into my life like a savior," she exclaims. "It was exciting for us to experience new, different things. We would play games like badminton and skipping. We read books, sang, and learnt that we had rights that we could use to live a better life." It was at the centre that Ekta first discovered her passion for kabaddi. The game gave her the same high that running did, and she took to it like a duck to water. Observing her enthusiasm and talent for the game, the facilitators at the centre encouraged Ekta to try out for PANI's kabaddi team. By this time, Ekta had determined that she would become a sportsperson. She understood that being selected to the team would help her receive professional coaching and access opportunities to compete, which would help her build a career in sports. So she decided to give it a shot.

Ekta's decision alarmed and displeased her grandmother. Kabaddi seemed like a rough, boisterous game to Dadi. She worried that her granddaughter's predilection for rough sports would prove to be a deterrent to good marriage alliances. Dadi was also concerned about Ekta sustaining injuries, particularly on her face, which would mar her looks. "I was constantly told that girls should not play sports," Ekta recalls with a cheeky grin. "Dadi believed I would become dark or get hurt, so I would not tell them much about the cuts and nicks I got while training. There were times when I sustained injuries on my face. It annoyed Dadi and she would complain that I could have hurt my eyes. I would tell her that's what medicines are for." Despite her enthusiasm and passion, Ekta's transition into being a sports player was as difficult for her as it was for her dadi. Having worn modest, voluminous clothes up until then, Ekta struggled to adapt to the sports shorts that revealed much of her hitherto covered legs. "It used to be very difficult for me to wear shorts," she recalls shyly. "I was always told to cover up and not show my skin or legs. So at first, I felt very shy and embarrassed to wear shorts because so much of my legs were revealed. I would only wear my shorts with tights beneath. It took me some time to find the courage to remove the tights."

Fortunately for Ekta, her grandfather delighted in her sporting achievements and encouraged her to pursue her passion for kabaddi. The air in Yadav Pur slowly started to change as the team began winning at different competitive events, including games at the state level. As the girls in the village started seeing Ekta's picture in the local newspapers, they were inspired to step out to play games and even sign up for PANI's sports training programmes. Ekta's dadu would keenly follow her matches, comforting her when her team lost and celebrating their wins. "When we lose, Dadu would ask me who we lost against and why," Ekta shares in a soft voice that belies her affection for her grandfather. "But when we win, I would find him reading the news with more interest because the newspapers would often carry our photos along with reports of our win."

Today, Ekta is the confident young woman she once dreamed of becoming. She firmly believes she can achieve anything she sets her mind to. The trophies she brings home and the publicity her team receives has wrought a change in even her dadi, who no longer grumbles as much when she sees Ekta set out for her training. Ekta is presently working towards obtaining a bachelor's degree in physical education. She hopes to become a well-known kabaddi player and eventually become a coach who will support girls and boys across Uttar Pradesh in achieving their sporting dreams. "Being a kabaddi player has changed my life," Ekta proclaims to everyone who will listen. "If not for my game, I would have remained in my home and village. But now, I have played at the state level, received trophies, medals, and certificates, and travelled to other places. I have been featured in the news. I feel proud of myself. One day, I will be on the television and make my family even prouder. I am confident of it."

# 15

## Never Give Up

*Diksha's unshakeable faith in herself fuels her to act and create positive
experiences that melt her family's resistance to her singing ambitions.*

**D**iksha Yadav was just a baby when she knew music was
going to be an important part of her life. Her older
sister often sang to her, and Diksha would lie in her
makeshift cradle, staring at her sister with large, goggling eyes
as she drank in the melodious singing in rapt silence. Maybe

this was how she knew she would become a singer before she could even form her first word.

Diksha's father, Hridayram, was a farmer in the village of Karaundi. He earned a modest income that sufficed to meet the needs of his family of seven. Theirs was a happy family. As the youngest of five siblings, Diksha was doted on by her mother, Vidya Devi, and her older siblings. But it was her third sister, the one who sang to her, to whom she felt the closest. As she grew up, young Diksha started to listen carefully and sing along. She wasn't very good at first, but that did not deter her. Singing was an immersive experience for her. The more she sang, the better she became. By the time Diksha entered her teenage years, her passion for music had grown to the point where she felt she could not survive a day without it. It often got her into trouble. She would be so immersed in listening to music as she did her chores around the house that she would miss hearing the calls of people who dropped by and be soundly scolded by her mother.

Diksha was deeply inspired by the popular Indian singer Neha Kakkar's rags to riches story. When she learnt that Neha Kakkar had found success on the famous reality show *The Indian Idol*, with no prior musical training, she was inspired to pursue a similar path. She enthusiastically sang at contests and school events, but unfortunately, her passion was often discounted by her family as a childish fancy. Diksha's family believed music was a risky profession. Every time Diksha tried telling her mother of her desperate wish to become a singer, she was fobbed off with examples of people whose careers and lives had been ruined by their pursuit of music. Vidya Devi would dissuade Diksha, asking her to choose a safer profession like teaching or medicine. But Diksha did not want to play it safe. Deep in her heart, she wanted to be famous for her singing—not just in Karaundi or Uttar Pradesh, but across India.

Diksha was away in Sultanpur completing her intermediate schooling when PANI opened its resource centre in Karaundi. While studying there, she fell sick and returned home. Hridayram subsequently refused to allow his youngest born to study away from home. As Diksha slowly settled back into life in Karaundi, she met Jyoti Upadhyay, who managed a cluster of PANI's centres. Those were the early days of the resource centre when the team was still trying to gain a foothold in the village. Karaundi was a very conservative village where adolescent girls were not allowed much freedom inside or outside their houses. Jyoti would often visit to speak to the villagers and allay their suspicions. The hostility of the villagers amused Diksha. "You know how it is," she shares cheekily. "When people are told about things that are good for their children but challenge their traditional mindsets, they react with suspicion. No matter how well meaning the advice is, the parents decide it will not benefit their children. Their real worry is that the children will become disobedient, unmanageable, and even question their parents."

Jyoti's feisty nature and her forthright ways appealed to Diksha. A friendship soon grew between the two young women. Fortunately for Diksha, the centre was close to her house, making it easy for her to sneak out quietly for visits. "I would look around carefully," she remembers with a gleeful chuckle. "If there was no one outside, I would quietly lift the latch on the gate and skip off down the road to the centre." Her antics exasperated Vidya Devi, who found it tedious to drop her chores to fetch Diksha from the centre as soon as she realised where she was. Jyoti too would often visit Diksha's home, and in time, Vidya Devi came to grudgingly accept Diksha's visits to the centre even though she grumbled about it. "Diksha is a girl who wanted to be more and do more," shares Jyoti. "She did not have much freedom. She wasn't allowed to wear anything other than salwars or visit her friends at home. She used to laugh as she told us that even if she were to wear a dress, she would be asked to wear pants with it and drape a *dupatta*.[33] Her parents meant well but they worried about neighbours gossiping."

As Diksha spent more time at the centre, she began to explore new possibilities for her life. She realised she had a right to her dreams and that it was okay for her to pursue them, even if it meant standing against her parents and the village at large. As her courage and confidence grew, Diksha also learnt to fight back against the village boys who harassed the girls walking or cycling on the village roads. The boys often went unchecked because the villagers firmly believed that "boys would be boys" and that it was up to the girls and their families to protect themselves from their

---

33 *Dupatta*: a long, shawl-like scarf traditionally worn by women on the Indian subcontinent to cover the head, face, and upper body.

testosterone-charged comments and harassment. Like the other village girls, Diksha had remained nonresponsive to derogatory comments or advances, fearing censure, criticism, and gossip. But now, she started to fight back fearlessly.

When Diksha completed her intermediate school and enrolled for graduation, she discovered she had more time on her hands. She decided to do a diploma programme in computer applications and followed it up with an advanced diploma. After consulting her father and brother, she decided to open a cybercafé in the village. At about this time, she received an opportunity from PANI to train as a singer in Faizabad. But Diksha had just set up her café, Jan Sewa Kendra, and was busy running it alongside her studies.[34] She knew her family's negative perceptions about singing meant that she would not receive permission to go to Faizabad for training, especially when they had just invested in her café. However, she did not give up on music and continued to sing at college functions, where her singing was applauded and even received favorable media coverage. She also received a few opportunities to host events as the master of ceremonies. Encouraged by the popular response, Diksha took to social media to share her music. "I must have been one of the first girls from my village to have a social presence," she shares proudly. "At first, I was scared and kept my social handles private. I would block anyone remotely connected to the village because I did not want any gossip about me. But now, my social

---

34 Jan Sewa Kendra: "A Centre That Serves People"

handles are public. Recently, when a boy tried to make derogatory insinuations about my character, I told him that I would break his fingers if he dared point them at me. Now he slinks away when he sees me coming from afar."

In early 2023, Diksha found an opportunity to audition online for a national singing competition. Unwilling to run the risk of being thwarted, she appeared quietly for it without sharing the news with her family. Much to her joy, she qualified for the second round and was asked to appear in person in Lucknow. At this point, she had no choice but to let her family know. Hridayram was astounded when he heard that his youngest daughter had auditioned for a singing competition; much to Diksha's surprise, he was neither angry nor discouraging. He merely asked her where she needed to go for the next round and when. Perhaps it was her growing popularity as a singer and the media appreciation, but Diksha's selection delighted Vidya Devi as well. Influenced by the rest of the family, Vidya Devi found herself encouraging Diksha to follow a dream she has carried with her since birth. Maybe they see her with new eyes because Diksha has proved to them that she can handle freedom responsibly. At nineteen, she owns and operates a profitable cybercafé alongside her studies. She takes care of her parents, ensuring they have their medications refilled, and helps in the fields as well. No matter what their reason is, Diksha now has the support of her family and she fearlessly forges ahead.

# 16

## Her Secret Dream

*Finding the courage to leave home to work in a faraway city
has helped Rehana think differently and dream big.*

Rehana Bano has a secret dream. She wants to, one day, own a famous boutique that will lure people from far and wide to buy the beautiful clothes she designs and stitches. It may seem like a pipe dream for a twenty-one-year-old Muslim girl from an obscure village in Uttar Pradesh. But

Rehana nurses her dream close to her heart. She knows she is only biding her time in her parents' home. One day, her family will find her a suitable husband and send her off to her real home—her husband's home—where she will have to care for a family of her own. Her mother did it as a young girl of sixteen. Her older sisters did so too. Rehana knows she will be the next to leave, either to be married or to pursue her dream.

Rehana has spent most of her life learning to be a good homemaker from her *ammi* and older sisters.[35] In the days before she came across PANI, she would cook, clean, watch over her younger siblings, and tend to the livestock on their land in the village of Purushottampur. It was a life she neither liked nor wanted. She went with the flow because she did not think she had the right to dream of a different life for herself. Rehana's father was a farmer who barely made enough to feed his large family of ten. Rehana went to school for a while but had to drop out in the ninth standard because of the family's financial struggles. "As a Muslim girl, I was expected to stay home and wait to be married off," she remembers. "My family used to say, 'What will you do with studies? You will marry and go to your in-laws' place anyway.'" So she lived a cloistered life within the confines of her home, honing her homemaking skills.

The only joy in Rehana's dreary existence was the time she spent at the old sewing machine at home, making clothes for

---

35 *Ammi*: mother; the noun or form of address for "mother" in Urdu and a few other Indian languages.

herself. Like most girls in Purushottampur, she rarely socialised. The menace of harassment and even abuse from the village boys made it almost impossible for them to step out of their houses. The restrictions on her movements felt unfair to Rehana. It angered her. But, on the rare occasions she ventured out, she seldom said anything to the boys who harassed her, worrying that a response would only invite more trouble. If she were to be embroiled in an altercation with them, word would quickly travel back home, and she would be harshly punished for disgracing herself.

Rehana came to know of PANI in 2019, when she heard of their back-to-school programme for adolescent girls. Her curiosity piqued, she enquired and discovered that, with PANI's support, she could in fact resume her studies without taxing her family's meagre financial resources. The prospect of going back to school worried Rehana. It had been three years since she dropped out. She felt she was now too old to go back. When Shyam Bahadur Verma and his colleague, Roshni, heard Rehana's concerns, they tried to assuage her fears. They assured her that while school may seem different at first, it would get easier as Rehana adjusted to the routine of going to school and studying. Shyam managed a cluster of PANI's centres in the region and identified a school close to Rehana's home in Purushottampur. Together with Roshni, he spoke to the teachers to request their support in helping Rehana adjust and acclimatise to school life and studying. Comforted by their support and encouragement, Rehana decided to give it her best shot. Unfortunately for Rehana, her parents were extremely resistant to the idea. When her father remained unmoved by her pleas, Rehana decided to seek Shyam's support. "It was exceedingly difficult to convince Rehana's father. Her mother was almost willing, but her father would not budge," Shyam recalls. "We tried telling him that the fees were taken care of and the proximity of the school to their home meant that Rehana could go and come very quickly. She only had to show up." Eventually, after numerous visits spanning a month, Shyam and Roshni were able to secure permission for Rehana to resume her studies.

Rehana enjoyed being back in school. She took to visiting PANI's centre, where she would have conversations with Shyam, Roshni, and their colleagues about her future. The discussions helped her realise that she wanted more from her life than marriage. She was tired of having to ask her parents for money for her expenses, and even more so of the questions that her requests inevitably provoked. The very idea of being financially independent was a revelation. She decided that she wanted to work, earn, and stand on her own feet. And thus, her dream of having a shop of her own was born. When Rehana successfully completed her intermediate schooling, the team at PANI helped her enroll in a tailoring skills development course at the Leprosy Mission's training centre in Masodha. She was elated when she secured a job with a garment manufacturer in Chennai upon completion of the course. It seemed that her dreams were slowly coming to life.

But Chennai was thousands of miles away, across the country. No one from her village had ever travelled to the south of

India before. This time, it was not just her family's resistance she had to contend with. The villagers of Purushottampur were outraged at the idea of an unmarried Muslim girl going so far away for work. "Rehana's father was willing to send her to Faizabad or any place closer to home but not to Chennai," remembers Shyam, who once again had to step in to persuade her parents. "We tried to assuage their concerns by telling them that Rehana would not be alone. Six other girls from her class, who were selected for jobs in Chennai, would be travelling, living, and working with her. We assured them that we would be involved and would intervene if there was any danger or trouble." But Rehana's family remained adamant. It was in vain that the team from PANI tried to explain to the family that while there were garment factories in Delhi and Noida offering jobs to girls, Chennai was the safer option. "We know of girls who went to Delhi to work as contract labor in garment factories and returned home in less than a week," explains Sima Verma, who manages and coordinates PANI's programmes for adolescent girls across Tarun. "Even though Chennai is so far away, it is safer." After weeks of concerted effort by Shyam, Sima, and Roshni, Rehana's parents reluctantly agreed to let her go to Chennai.

Unfortunately for Rehana, Chennai proved to be a disappointment. She struggled to adapt to the city's food, climate, language, and culture. Her job made it even more difficult for her to acclimatise to the change. Despite working in a big company, she was tasked with stitching labels onto T-shirts and was required to stitch as many as one hundred and thirty labels in an hour. Failure to do so resulted in her being harshly scolded. Rehana would frequently call Shyam to share her struggles, and he would urge her to give herself time to get used to the job, city, people, and culture, reminding her of the challenges she had had to overcome to get there. But for Rehana, the struggle was real. The rice-based meals popular in South India did not agree with her. The curries tasted foreign to her palate. To make matters worse, the people were not friendly or welcoming. Every time Rehana and her friends went to buy groceries at the local *kirana* stores,[36] the shopkeepers would grimace and pull faces hearing them speak in Hindi.[37] "When I was placed with the garment company in Chennai, I was very happy," she recalls. "I was determined to do well. But Chennai was too different from home. I thought to myself that the reason I want to work is so that I can live well. What is the point of working and earning if I am unhappy, struggling, and not even being able to eat?"

Rehana eventually returned to Purushottampur, planning to find a job closer to home. Her dream continues to hold her in its thrall. Her sojourn in Chennai was an adventure that has made her not only wiser but clearer and more resolute in her pursuit of her dream. She now knows how to navigate her way around new situations and people. She has also learnt the importance

---

36 *Kirana* stores: small grocery or general supplies stores found in neighbourhoods
37 Hindi: one of India's twenty-two official languages that is popularly spoken across North India. India has over 120 major languages and more than 1,500 dialectic variations.

of being inclusive. "When people from different places come to my shop speaking different languages, I will remember to make the effort to be friendly," she shares with a smile. "I will look them in the eye and make them feel like they matter." Her words belie the fact that she is on a journey. It is no longer just a dream she pursues but a goal that is now more within reach than ever before.

# 17

## Break Down the Doors

*The gleam and ambition in Shivangi's eyes show the world
that the most important doors she has broken through are the ones
that still keep her mother imprisoned.*

Shivangi breaks down doors. Doors that keep her safely ensconced within a suffocating cocoon, woven by her family from the diktats and controls of society. Frissons of restrained anger roll off her words, like steam hissing off a hot griddle, when she emphatically pronounces, "We are like princesses in old fairy tales who are locked away behind many formidable doors. We must break them down to be free." You cannot help but wonder why this young waiflike girl feels as strongly as she does, or even where her anger comes from. That is, until she explains, "If twenty-five-year-old girls in our country are struggling to find ways to build a career, then the need is not to open doors but to break them down." It is only then that the penny drops. Her emotions stem from her own experiences of having had doors slammed shut in her face. These are doors to opportunities that should have been open because girls have passed through them before. Unfortunately, they remain closed, keeping millions like Shivangi on the outside.

Shivangi spent her early childhood in Punjab, where her father, Ram Akbar, worked with a private company. He was the sole income earner in their small family and made just about enough to make ends meet. Her mother, Sindhu, was a homemaker who had been married at the tender age of seven and had centered her life around her husband ever since. Sindhu believed her daughter would one day be a devoted wife and mother like her. Perhaps it would have been so if Shivangi had not been asked by her teacher about her dream for herself. She was barely seven years old, and the question puzzled her because she did not know what it meant to dream. The women in her family had never gone to school, and the men had not studied past the tenth standard. It was when the teacher pointed out her proficiency in science, and suggested that she could become a doctor, that Shivangi found her first dream.

Shivangi moved back to their village, Barehata, with her mother and brother, after completing the fourth standard, and continued her studies in the local village school. She was still in school when PANI set up its resource centre at Barehata. Shivangi enjoyed visiting the centre and the discussions she had there. On one occasion, when the girls were asked about their dreams for themselves, Shivangi confidently shared that she wanted to become a doctor but did not know how to. Her mother did not take her dream seriously. In fact, Sindhu was convinced that Shivangi would not pass her tenth standard board exam and was shocked when she scored the highest marks in the village. "Mummy did not believe me when I told her that I had scored 82 percent and stood first in the whole village," she shares with a sad smile. "I was so excited to tell her, but she was skeptical and believed it only after our neighbours checked my marks independently."

The relationship between a mother and daughter tends to be tenuously empowering or fractiously disempowering. Despite their blood bond, their experiences at a particular age are rooted in different times, and the ever-changing world often makes it necessary for a mother to challenge her own conditioning and life script to be able to support her daughter's dreams. Unfortunately, Sindhu was not willing to do so. Despite the excellent results, Sindhu urged Shivangi to study arts at an intermediate school near their home, so that she could come and go easily. Shivangi, on the other hand, was keen to study science in a school located farther away, where she believed she would receive a more qualitative education. "We think our families are right all the time, but this is not always true, especially in families like mine, where education levels are low," she shares candidly. "I learnt that it is important for me to use my voice to speak up for what I know is right for me." Her persistence won the day.

Shivangi was often at loggerheads with her mother, who had very definite ideas about how girls should dress and behave and tried to force them on Shivangi. When Shivangi fought back to be her own person, Sindhu would furiously complain to Meenakshi Dwivedi, who managed PANI's resource centres in and around Barehata, and demand to know what they were teaching Shivangi at the centre. When Shivangi completed her intermediate schooling, she had the opportunity to study fashion design at a Government Polytechnic far away from home. She was excited, but her mother was determined to enroll her for her graduate studies at the nearest college. It was not what Shivangi wanted. She wanted to either study fashion design or sign up for coaching for the medical school entrance exams. But Sindhu would have none of it. She was determined to dissuade Shivangi from becoming a doctor, pointing out that their financial situation would not stretch to cover the fees of her medical courses. When the battle between mother and daughter reached an impasse, Sindhu pressed for a truce, promising to enroll Shivangi for the state medical entrance coaching after she had graduated. Seeing no way around the fait accompli her mother presented her with, Shivangi decided to grit her teeth and accept her mother's terms.

Shivangi was deeply concerned when she realised that Sindhu planned to marry her off by the time she completed her graduation. She was barely twenty and not ready for marriage. "I wanted to achieve a lot," she shares. "I felt it would not happen if I were to marry someone whose thinking centered around only putting three meals on the table. Most of the prospects my parents found had studied no further than tenth standard or intermediate school. I am a graduate. Why would I marry someone who is not at least a graduate?" The pressure began to mount as Shivangi rejected one prospective groom after the other. Shivangi realised that when it came to marriage alliances, it was normal for a boy to reject a girl he found unsuitable, without having to explain his decision. But a girl needed to have a very good reason to reject a suitor her family found worthy. Angered by Shivangi's continual rejection of suitable alliances, Sindhu complained bitterly to Meenakshi and even asked her to intervene. But Meenakshi had borne witness to Shivangi's struggles and heartache over the years and continued to encourage her to do what was right for her.

When Shivangi graduated, Sindhu once again dissuaded her from joining coaching  by pushing her to enroll in a master's programme. Angered by her mother's deception and terrified of being forced into marriage, Shivangi decided to take matters into her own hands. Encouraged by Meenakshi and her colleagues, Shivangi found herself a teaching job at a school nearby and explored courses and programmes related to medicine. She was delighted when she found a modestly priced operation theater technician's course in Faizabad that she could join. But when she tried talking to Sindhu about going to Faizabad to pursue this, her mother once again tried to discourage her, citing their inability to afford the fees. At her wits' end, Shivangi eventually borrowed money from a friend to enroll in the programme, knowing that she was risking her mother's fury and displeasure. "My mother was so completely against my studying and working that she did everything she could to stop me," Shivangi shares, the pain palpable in her voice. "She refused to accept money from me when I was working as a teacher, saying, 'Are we to eat from your earnings now?' My father is happy when I do things to make my dreams come true. But my mother thinks he does not like me going out or doing things, so she keeps putting obstacles in my way."

Recognising that Sindhu was unlikely to support her, Shivangi decided to use her savings to move to Faizabad to study and work. The distance hasn't deterred her mother, who continues to harangue her for various reasons, including marriage. As painful and exhausting as it is, Shivangi refuses to bow down to her mother's demands. "There is so much I want to achieve in life," she states with determination. "If my mother had supported me even a little, I would have done well. But I take challenges in my stride and move on." At twenty-three,

Shivangi continues to forge ahead, breaking down the doors that stand between her and her dreams. One hopes that she will, one day, be able to break down the door that closes her mother's heart to her achievements and dreams.

# 18

# The Trailblazer

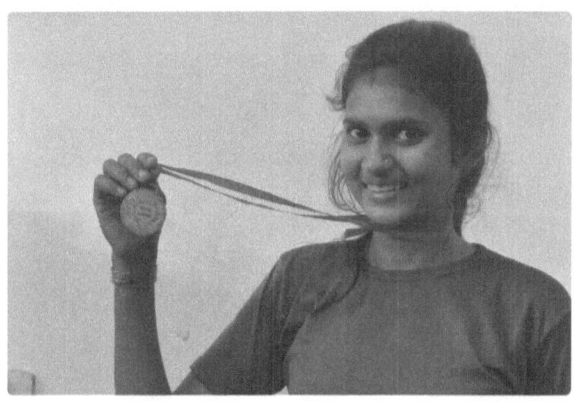

*A champion on and off the field, Nilakshi is determined to support young women in pursuing their goals, so they do not feel alone or afraid.*

Menarche for the average Indian girl is seldom a private biological experience. It is a milestone that announces to her family, and sometimes the community, that her body has come of childbearing age. In villages across Uttar Pradesh, a girl's first period is a gateway into the world of secrecy, shame, and taboos that shroud the female body. It is a segregated world, more intricately layered than a delicate French pastry, that is crafted from draconian rules, fear, shame, and pregnant silences and presided over by an implacable matriarch or two. In Nilakshi's home, it was her eighty-year-old dadi who shaped and controlled this inner world of women and girls.

Nilakshi lived in a joint family in the village of Gurauli. Her father, Jagadamba Prasad, worked as a daily wage earner at a local *agarbatti* company.[38] Her mother, Poonam, spent her days working in the fields and managing the needs of their large family. Nilakshi was a lanky, carefree child who loved playing at school and home. However, the fun and games came to an end with her first period. She was already in her teens, and menarche prompted her dadi to determinedly set about the task of domesticating Nilakshi. She was strictly forbidden from playing games, hanging out with friends after school, or lingering outdoors for any reason. Like other adolescent girls in Gurauli, Nilakshi would leave the house only to go to school or to work in the fields. It seemed like her dadi's eagle eyes were perennially on her, making sure she was walking, talking, and behaving with feminine modesty. Nilakshi restlessly chafed against her grandmother's restrictions, but she had no choice other than to submit. It was pointless for her to

---

38 *Agarbatti*: incense or joss sticks that are thin, wooden sticks coated in a fragrant mixture of herbs, resins, and oils and burnt for fragrance

appeal to her mother. Poonam had been long bent into compliance by her mother-in-law and had forsaken her words.

The placid flow of everyday life in Gurauli was disrupted when PANI set up its resource centre in the village. The villagers were suspicious of the centre and its planned activities. So when Anjali Pandey, in whose cluster the Garauli centre fell, came calling at Nilakshi's home, she was met with skepticism and veiled hostility. No matter what the other girls in the village chose to do, Nilakshi's dadi was vehemently opposed to her granddaughter visiting the centre. But much to Nilakshi's delight, Anjali was able to convince Poonam and Jagadamba Prasad and secure permission for Nilakshi and her sisters to visit the centre. "When I went to the centre for the first time, I was happy to see the girls playing games," Nilakshi recalls with a sunny smile. "I was careful to tell my mother about all that I saw, did, and experienced at the centre because I wanted her to be more comfortable with my visits. Slowly she started to object lesser and lesser when I set out for the centre."

Nilakshi's aptitude for games soon won her a spot in PANI's competitive athletics training programme. The selection surprised her. She had never imagined that her childhood passion for games could one day become a profession to pursue. At sixteen, she was enthused by the possibilities of becoming a well-known athlete and made up her mind to take the opportunity that fate had presented her with. Nilakshi knew her plans would not go down well with her family, particularly her grandmother. She was right. Her dadi was enraged when Nilakshi broached the subject at home and sought permission from her parents to travel to Tarun for training. With her dadi demanding that Nilakshi's movements outside the house be curbed at once, Nilakshi frantically pleaded with Poonam to intercede with her father on her behalf. Her impassioned pleas moved her parents, and they reluctantly granted her permission. "My family was not happy," she recalls. "I had permission, but there was no one to encourage or support me. The prospect of cycling alone to Tarun scared me. It was often dark when I left home, and the roads would be empty. Since there was no one I could talk to about my fears, I would tell myself that if I want to achieve something, then I must do it by myself."

As Nilakshi gradually adapted to training, her life began to slowly change in ways she had never imagined possible. In pursuing a dream, she was unwittingly blazing a new trail through the fabric of her village. She soon realised that her grandmother was not the only person who was alarmed and infuriated by the freedom she enjoyed. Her early morning trips to Tarun, and her comings and goings in general, had not escaped the women of Gurauli. The village grapevine had already begun to hum and buzz. Before long, the gossiping women were haranguing Poonam. "Why do you give your daughter so much freedom? What will she gain from this sports training?" they would demand to know, prophesying darkly that Nilakshi was running wild and would come to a bad end. Poonam was crushed, but her daughter's happy face prompted her to shrug off the vicious complaints. However, when the girls in the village started to take their cue from Nilakshi and move freely outside their houses, the alarmed women intensified their vitriolic attacks. It was only a matter of time before the gossip, harassment, and social pressure drove Poonam to a breaking point, prompting her to urge Nilakshi to give up her training.

Those were difficult days for Nilakshi. She was only sixteen and had to contend with the anger of an entire village of women. Even though the tide of public opinion was against her, Nilakshi remained resolute in the pursuit of her dream. Things came to a head one day, when Nilakshi was returning home with a friend. As the girls stood by the roadside, exchanging pleasantries before they parted ways, they were accosted and teased by a group of village boys. Angered by the unprovoked comments and harassment, Nilakshi fiercely berated the boys. And thus, a scandal was born. The villagers were horrified at the audacity of a young girl who not only provoked comments from boys but also quarreled with them on the streets in broad daylight. When the news reached home, her parents were ashamed and angered. In their eyes, Nilakshi had dishonoured the family. She was immediately grounded.

The news dismayed Vikram Veer Singh, who managed PANI's competitive sports and athletics programmes. A burly, jovial man, Vikram was a common sight at the training grounds, where he would often tease, cheer, and guide the girls as they trained. He was aware that each girl in the programme had to surmount great challenges to show up for training day after day. "It really is not easy for the girls," he remarks. "They struggle to adapt to the training attire at first. They need to cycle long distances to reach Tarun. They have to learn to ignore the looks and comments of passersby as they train. It is a lot for fifteen- and sixteen-year-olds to juggle school, household chores, and fieldwork and brave the censure of their neighbours to come to training. We do our best to offer them support and reassurance."

Vikram's sympathies were with Nilakshi, but he knew that they had to let the dust settle on the scandal.

When Nilakshi had missed her training for over a month, Vikram and Anjali decided to intervene. Anjali set out for Nilakshi's home, preparing herself to pacify Jagadamba Prasad and Poonam and seek permission for Nilakshi to resume her training. Ironically, at this time, the women in Nilakshi's neighbourhood, who had been her most vociferous critics, found themselves in need of her help to run errands. They approached Poonam seeking permission for Nilakshi to be allowed out of the house again. Thus, when Anjali came calling, she was pleasantly surprised to find Jagadamba Prasad and Poonam more amenable to the idea of Nilakshi resuming her training.

It has been two years since the scandal. Nilakshi is eighteen and has already notched up a stack of medals and trophies. Her eyes are trained on winning national-level track and field athletic events. Her vision is clear in her mind's eye. She will become a nationally known athlete and eventually a sports coach. Nilakshi now walks in Gurauli with confidence. She is not afraid to speak up for herself, her sisters, or the girls in the village who live with greater freedom because of her. "I want my sister to have the support I did not have," Nilakshi confides. "I tell her that she can tell me anything and count on me. I want this for all girls in my village." She pauses to consider for a moment, before adding, "Standing alone is difficult and painful. We girls must learn to support each other so we live better lives." Perhaps she is already dreaming of new trails to blaze through the village of Gurauli.

# 19

## Why Not Girls?

Deepa was in her early teens when she lost her father. The tragic loss was a blow for her mother, Mala, who had to, all at once, assume the mantle of bread-winner for her family of five. However, Mala's troubles went beyond single parenting or figuring out finances. A woman without a husband is perceived differently, often unkindly and rapaciously, by a patriarchal society. The loss of her husband changed Mala's status in their village, Charawa. The respectability and security that marriage provided vanished overnight, leaving her to gingerly pick her way around new family dynamics and harsher societal perceptions. Finding sustainable work that paid enough to meet the family's needs was difficult, but Mala worked hard as a hired farmhand and picked up odd jobs when she could. Theirs was a difficult life. By the time Deepa completed her tenth standard, Mala was impoverished and unable to educate her further. She had married off her two older children and was barely making ends meet. Her father, Deepa's *nana*,[39] who was the titular head of the family and often the deciding voice in familial matters of importance, discouraged Mala from educating Deepa further. He believed women needed just enough education to make good marriages. However, Deepa was tired of living in abject poverty and had very different plans for herself. She wanted to become a doctor and earn an honourable living by serving others. But like most other girls in Charawa, Deepa had very little freedom to dream or pursue dreams.

It was at this time that PANI opened their resource centre in Charawa. Mala was extremely suspicious when PANI's team members called on her to invite Deepa to the centre. Believing there was no real benefit to the association, she refused to let Deepa go over to the centre. Fortunately for Deepa, the women of PANI refused to give up on her. They would visit her home frequently to explain their work and activities, hoping to assuage Mala's fears. In time, Mala came to trust the team and permitted Deepa to visit. It proved to be a turning point in Deepa's life. The sessions and conversations she had there were unlike any she had experienced before. "It was the first time in my life that I thought about girls having the right to live and do things as boys do," she shares. "Take for instance, the fact that boys can

---

39 *Nana*: maternal grandfather; the proper noun or form of address for the maternal grandfather in Hindi and many other Indian languages

go out whenever they want to. No one scolds a boy who comes home at nine or ten o'clock at night, but a girl who is out of the house even during the day is scolded severely and punished."

Deepa felt suffocated when she thought about the nuances of inequality and the different ways girls are discriminated against in everyday life. She would often think of her thwarted dream of becoming a doctor and wonder out loud to Mala, "Why are girls treated differently than boys?" Unwilling to give up on her dream, Deepa decided to resume her studies with financial aid from PANI. She enrolled herself in the eleventh standard, but even with the scholarship, it was difficult to meet the expenses of her schooling. This time, Deepa was determined not to give up. She started working alongside her mother in the fields after school to raise money for her tuition. It was exhausting, but she needed the money and ploughed on. "People used to ask my mother why she was making me work in the fields at such a young age," Deepa shares with disarming candor, "but I did not feel bad. I was willing to do what it took to ensure that I stayed in school." By the time Deepa completed intermediate school, she was already exploring ways to become employable. Encouraged by the team at the centre, she decided to enroll in a spoken English course in Faizabad and leverage the institute's placement services to find a job.

Her decision caused a furor at home. Mala was aghast at the idea of Deepa moving to Faizabad to study. It was not a done thing for the girls in their village. As a single parent, Mala was acutely aware of the eyes of the village constantly boring through the walls of their little home to scrutinise the way she and her daughters conducted themselves. Mala also worried about how Deepa would manage by herself away from home, what kind of people she would meet, and most importantly, if the sudden freedom would cause her to go astray. More than anything else, Mala dreaded the reactions of her son and her father. Her fears were not in vain. Deepa's brother was extremely resistant to the idea of his sister leaving home, even when it meant that the family could finally alleviate their poverty. For him, family honour was far more important, and he did not trust his sister to conduct herself with dignity. Fortunately for Deepa, her brother lived away from them, which allowed her to focus on convincing Mala. "I asked my mother, 'How long will we live like this in poverty and hardship?'" she recalls. "My mother was struggling to provide for my younger sister and me. I explained that if I learn a skill and get a job, our lives will change because I can send money to her." Mala eventually agreed and even persuaded Deepa's brother. But it was not an easy decision for Mala to make. She was frequently besieged by neighbours who would make pointed remarks about her having let Deepa leave home for studies. Things came to a head when Deepa completed her course and was asked to appear for interviews in Delhi. This time, Mala was far more willing to let Deepa go, even though she knew she would have to contend with the displeasure of the menfolk and the vicious gossip of the neighbours.

Deepa's grandfather furiously berated Mala when he heard

the news. He had been greatly displeased that Mala allowed Deepa to study in Faizabad. When he heard of her plans to travel to Delhi for interviews and subsequently move there for work, he threatened to disown his daughter and granddaughters. Deepa's brother was also hostile and went as far as to tell his mother that he would have nothing to do with them if Deepa left for Delhi. But Deepa was not willing to back down. She pointed out to her brother that all the girls in her class came from villages around Faizabad and were attending interviews, so why not her? "I could see that my brother was worried about me living alone in the city," Deepa reveals. "We both knew that if the villagers talk badly about me, it will affect my sisters as well." Recognising her brother's deep trust issues, she urged him to contemplate a better outcome: What if she went to Delhi and brought honour to the family? Deepa's brother grudgingly capitulated in the face of her calm, irrefutable logic. It was thus that Deepa came to Delhi to work for a company that made power window switches for automobiles.

Life as a working girl in the big city has changed Deepa. She has traded her conservative salwar suits for jeans, T-shirts, and dresses. She is more confident and can interact easily with people, particularly men and boys. She is unafraid to step out at night to run errands. "The girls at my hostel keep saying that things have changed ever since my friends and I moved in," she shares with a gleeful laugh. "Before we came, the girls would not step out after sunset. But once they saw us go out at eight or nine o'clock at night to run chores or errands, they followed suit." Deepa is only nineteen years old and much to her joy, she is already able to send money home to her mother. She intends to save and resume her education, for she believes that she will be a doctor one day. There was a time when she used to think that dreams were a privilege reserved for boys. But now she asks, *why not girls?*

# 20

## So What If I Have a Daughter?

*By supporting her father in providing for their family, Kushboo challenges mindsets by taking on responsibilities that are traditionally deemed a son's to perform.*

All her life, Kushboo yearned to have an older brother. Most of the girls in her village, Sihipur, had older brothers who would manage the fields, go to the market and bank, and work to support their families. But in her family, she was the eldest and often had to step up to support her mother as a son would have. Her sisters and brother were considerably younger. While growing up, Kushboo would go to school and upon returning home take care of her siblings and the house, making it possible for her parents, Sukhiram and Reema, to work in their fields. Kushboo was still in school when Sukhiram decided to work as an ATM security guard in Delhi and moved to the city with Reema and the younger children. Unable to afford Kushboo's education in the city, the family was forced to leave her behind with her grandparents to continue her schooling.

Reema returned to Sihipur when the younger children were ready to start school. With her father away, the responsibility of supporting her mother and younger siblings fell to Kushboo. Sihipur was an extremely conservative village where young girls were not permitted much freedom outside of their homes. Every time Kushboo stepped out of the house to buy things in the market or visit the bank, she would have to contend with the critical looks and censure of the villagers. As she grew into adolescence, Kushboo became increasingly aware of the dire financial conditions of her family as well as the immense pressure upon her father as the sole breadwinner. Not knowing how to help, she often found herself wishing for an older brother who could work and alleviate some of her father's stress.

Upon completion of her intermediate schooling, Kushboo enrolled for her graduation. It was a time when PANI was actively working in Sihipur to support the empowerment of girls. As Kushboo attended meetings at PANI's resource centre and interacted with members of their team, she began engaging in conversations about women's rights, particularly their right to an education and to work. It made a deep impression on her, and she found herself toying with the idea of getting a job and contributing to her family's finances. She soon found an opportunity to enroll in a skills development course and decided to broach the subject with her parents. But both Sukhiram and Reema were not enthusiastic about the idea. They were unsure if Kushboo would be safe if she were allowed to live away from home. The girls in their village never went out to study or work. Reema was particularly concerned about what people would say if they allowed Kushboo to leave home. With Sukhiram away in Delhi, she and her children were constantly scrutinised by the people of Sihipur. Reema worried that the villagers would gossip viciously about Kushboo and her. But Kushboo refused to be discouraged. She persistently tried to persuade her mother, so much so that Reema started to complain to PANI's team members when they came calling on the family. "This girl does not let me sleep in peace," she would say. "She is so adamant about this skills development course and working, but how do we let her go so far away from home alone?"

Kushboo kept trying relentlessly to convince her parents that there was no cause for worry because she would not be alone and that there would be many other girls joining her. But as time went by without her father showing any sign of granting permission, Kushboo began to worry that she would lose this opportunity. "I would ask my mother, what will we do if this opportunity vanishes?" she recalls with a big smile. "What if I lose this chance and never get another? After pestering my mother for three or four months, she finally agreed and decided to speak in my favor to my father."

With Reema on her side, it was only a matter of time before Sukhiram relented and allowed Kushboo to enroll in a skills development course. When the villagers heard that Kushboo was leaving home to study and maybe even work, the whole of Sihipur buzzed with gossip and criticism. "We used to feel bad," Reema says about that time. "The people used to talk so badly, and we had no choice but to ignore it. There is a saying that the dogs will bark but the elephant keeps walking on. That is how we were when Kushboo had to first go away to study and then to Noida to work."

Upon completion of her programme, Kushboo went to Noida with her classmates and tutors to look for a job. It was her first time in a city, and Kushboo found it very difficult to adapt. The gully she lived in was cramped, crowded, dirty, and very different from the village where there was space, fresh air, fields, and quiet. Kushboo felt very unsafe and scared those first few weeks in the city. She even wondered if she had made a mistake. But with support and encouragement from her tutors, she was able to assuage her fears and do well in her interviews. "Our trainers would keep telling us to trust ourselves and answer to the best of our abilities," she recalls. "Their encouragement gave me confidence. I did not feel disadvantaged because I came from the village. I realised that whether we come from the city or village, it is our skills and hard work that matters."

Kushboo eventually got a job at a call centre, where she often had to handle angry and rude customers. For a girl who used to tremble and shake at the thought of talking to people, this was a job that caused her great angst and stress day after day. Sometimes she would end her day in tears because of angry and rude customers. But when her supervisor advised her to shake off the customers' anger and rudeness and move on, Kushboo realised that it was not personal. She was increasingly able to deal with it without being affected. As the days passed, Kushboo learnt to adapt to the city despite her early difficulties. The girls from her village who accompanied her to Noida struggled to adapt to the restrictive space of the hostel and its stringent rules. Many of them eventually gave up and returned home. Kushboo, however, held on, remembering her responsibilities as the oldest child and the fact that her family did not have the financial means to offer her such opportunities over and over.

Today, Kushboo is an inspiration for the girls of Sihipur, particularly those who have dropped out of school and are at home. As the first girl from her village to work in the city, she is a role model who has prompted many girls in Sihipur, and their mothers who once criticised and gossiped about her, to seek her advice and suggestions. Kushboo, however, holds no grudges and is happy to share her insights, experiences, and learnings with them. Now that she knows she can take care of herself, she aspires to study nursing and pursue her dream of working in a hospital. "If I had an older brother, things would have been easier for me and my father," she says with calm confidence. "As the oldest child, I do my best to take care of my family and ease my father's burden. My priority is to ensure that my siblings are educated and working and that my parents are well provided for. I hope my father feels, *So what if I have a daughter? She supports me just as a son would.*"

# 21

## Dolls and Dreams

*Nandini's refusal to give up on her dream of becoming a singer gradually converted her brother, Arun, from being her harshest critic to her strongest ally.*

Come August and households across Uttar Pradesh begin to twinkle and shine as an array of festivals loom large on the horizon. These are mostly grand affairs involving fasting and feasting in equal measure. Among the smaller festivals tucked into the folds of the holy month, Shravan,[40] is Nag Panchami,[41] a festival that honours serpents as the celestial guardians of gods, monks, and family lineages. On the morning of Nag Panchami, women gird their hungry fasting bellies to scour their homes and prepare sacred offerings. For little girls, however, it is a day for doll making. Like little mice, they excitedly burrow through their mothers' old saris to salvage scraps of cloth that their tender little fingers can nimbly twine, wind, and tie into doll shapes. They gently tut-tut to themselves in frustration when the fabric refuses to heed the silent urging of their fingers as they shape, pin, sew, and decorate their dolls, and they exclaim joyfully when it does heed them. Once they are done, the girls race out to show their dolls to their friends. They then make their way to the village *chauraha*,[42] laughing and chattering, to hang their dolls for all to see. Sadly, their joy is ephemeral. For they are soon followed by their brothers brandishing decorated sticks who fall upon the dolls and beat them to tatters. From dolls to dreams, a girl's brother can crush both with ease in the villages of Uttar Pradesh. It is how things are and have been done for generations. But in the village of Ghuritikar, two siblings, Nandini and Arun, are breaking from tradition

---

40 *Shravan*: a holy month in the lunar-based Hindu calendar which is marked by fasting, prayers, and religious festivals

41 *Nag Panchami*: a festival dedicated to the snake gods, or the Nagas, celebrated on the first day after the new moon in Shravan

42 *Chauraha*: crossroads

as they pursue a dream Nandini has carried with her since she was six years old.

Nandini stumbled upon her dream for her life by chance. It happened in the third standard. Her teacher one day decided to engage the class in a game of *antakshari*.[43] Nandini's singing enchanted her teacher so much that she could not stop talking about it and prompted others to listen to her. As Nandini sang the same song over and over, Nandini started to see herself with new eyes. She felt special, that she had a unique gift, and she knew, one day, she would become a well-known singer. Nandini's family was indulgent when she told them about her wonderful day at school, but they did not take her declarations of becoming a singer seriously. Her older sister also sang well. But good girls from respectable families did not sing or dance in public, and the family did not treat it as a gift to nurture or profession to pursue. Nandini's father, Maya Ram, worked as a laborer away from their home. His earnings were meagre, and the family of five frequently struggled to make ends meet. Nandini's mother, Shobhawati Devi, was keen that she studied well. Shobhawati herself had not received an education as a child and was married very young. "I went to school for a few days," she recalls wistfully. "Something bad happened in my family soon after I started school. People felt it was because I was sent to school, and so my studies ended within days of

---

43 *Antakshari*: a popular singing game in India where the players take turns to sing the first verse of a song that begins with the consonant alphabet at the end of the previous contestant's song

starting." Shobhawati Devi was therefore determined to educate Nandini as much as their finances permitted.

Despite her family's lukewarm response, Nandini continued to hold her dream of becoming a singer close to her heart. Her teachers encouraged her to sing at every opportunity, and Nandini soon became a popular face at the school's singing and dancing competitions. She hit a rocky road when she entered adolescence. Her brother, Arun, who had always been discouraging, started to vehemently object to her participating in the singing and dancing competitions. With their father away, Arun was deemed the man of the house, and he worried about the reputation his sister would acquire if she kept singing in public. "People look at girls who sing and dance in a very bad way," he explains. "The problem is in their perception, but I did not want my sister to be spoken badly of by my friends or any other people in the village." Arun made it a point to often tell Nandini that her passion for singing was pointless. At about the same time, Nandini also started to notice that her friends and other older girls were being discouraged by their families and the school from dancing or singing on the stage. However, Nandini's excellent singing prompted the principal to allow her to continue singing on stage, encouraging her to pursue it even after completing her tenth standard.

Unfortunately, the COVID-19 pandemic made her family's financial position precarious. Thousands of daily wage-earning laborers struggled to find work during the lockdowns. Maya Ram was one of them. As the family's income dwindled to a trickle, Nandini was forced to discontinue her studies. She felt she had to support her family by acquiring skills that would make her employable rather than pursue her dream of becoming a singer. Those were difficult days for her. On one hand, she was gripped by a dream she did not know how to achieve, and on the other hand, she was constrained by the family's financial situation and Arun's objections. "I felt completely broken," she recalls. "There was no one to support me or guide me. My didi is an excellent singer and her talent was not acknowledged. I felt, *If my sister who sang better than me could not become a singer, then what chance did I have?*"

It was at this critical juncture that her path led her to PANI. Like many of the villagers, Nandini and her family were skeptical of the centre in Ghuritikar and its mission of empowering adolescent girls. Nandini's interest was piqued when the didis from PANI kept coming over to talk about their activities and programmes. She started visiting the centre, where she met girls from other centres who were pursuing sports, learning new skills, or working already. It filled her with new hope. Nandini decided to resume her studies with PANI's support and enrolled in intermediate school. When the PANI team realised that Nandini was very serious about becoming a singer, they decided to support her. Together, they identified an experienced music school in Faizabad where Nandini could begin her training as a singer.

Her sister was delighted when she heard of the opportunity Nandini had to train as a singer. Her parents were less so. Unable to refuse in the face of Nandini's joy and excitement,

Maya Ram reluctantly agreed to permit her if the rest of the family agreed. Arun, however, objected fiercely and vociferously. The social stigma attached to women in professions involving singing, dancing, and entertainment weighed heavily upon him. He was concerned that if Nandini were to go to Faizabad, his friends and the villagers would speak badly of her and their family. In a bid to assuage the family's concerns, Shyam Bahadur Verma, who managed a cluster of centres around Ghuritikar, sought to have conversations with Arun and Maya Ram. "I told both of them that Nandini has an uncommon gift that we must nurture," Shyam recalls. "I assured them that she would be training in singing only, not dancing, and that Arun was welcome to come to Faizabad with their mother to see the music school and her dormitory." Nandini worked relentlessly to persuade her brother, pointing out that her role models were singers like Lata Mangeshkar, who was revered the world over as Bollywood's most beloved voice, and Neha Kakkar, who herself had risen from poverty because of her singing. Her earnest pleading eventually changed her brother's mind, and, to her delight, made him her greatest champion. Today, Arun manages a YouTube channel for Nandini's music and badgers her for recordings of her songs to share on social media. "I used to stop Nandini from pursuing her singing, worrying about what people would say about her and our family," he reveals, embarrassment creasing his young face, "but people had good things to say, and it made me feel very proud. Now I do everything I can to support her."

At sixteen, Nandini is on her way to living her dream. She

plans to major in music after intermediate school. "Fighting for my dream changed me and my family," she shares joyfully. "I thought I could not fend for myself if I went out. But now my parents and I know I can. My family's support has been the greatest change." She was delighted when twelve girls from her village followed her lead and enrolled at her music school. Her eyes sparkle with anticipation as she looks ahead to the day when her name and voice will inspire thousands across the country to follow their singing dreams. "I am sure, one of these days, one or more of the videos on my YouTube channel will go viral," she shares with a grin at Arun, knowing here is a brother who will nurture her dolls and dreams.

# 22

## Born to Win

*Shalu's medals are a testimonial to her focus on working hard, winning, and one day achieving her dream of being an Olympian.*

t is six o'clock on a Sunday morning. The first rays of the day fall upon the women and girls in village households around Tarun, urging them to bestir themselves, rub the sleep out of their still-tired eyes, and light their *chulhas*[44] to brew the fami-

---

44  *Chulha*: a traditional U-shaped mud cooking stove used for indoor cooking in villages

ly's first cups of tea. But not all girls are brewing tea or setting about their morning chores. Some are frantically cycling down the dusty village roads towards the *kutcha*[45] ground in Tarun that is already teeming with scores of young, chattering girls dressed in blue. They all are track and field athletes supported by PANI, ready to begin their day's training.

Shalu, who has woken up at 5:00 a.m. to cycle in from Pichaura village, warms up quietly on the sidelines. She is a slight, petite girl whose demeanor gives away her grit, resilience, and determination to excel. Although her games of choice are the 100-meter dash and javelin throw, over the next two hours she will train for all the athletic events. It is no small wonder that, at seventeen, Shalu is already a local celebrity who has won a host of medals and trophies at block and state sporting events. Her hero is Neeraj Chopra, the Indian star track and field athlete, and like him, she hopes to bring home an Olympic medal one day.

Being an Olympian is an ambitious goal for a young girl from an impoverished family in the rural innards of India, where facilities and opportunities are both scarce. But there was a time when Shalu neither had any dreams nor even knew how to dream. Her mother, Sheela, had been married when she was only eight. Shalu believed that she too would eventually be married to a suitor of her parents' choice. Back in those days, Shalu was a content child even though she lived a sheltered

---

45 *Kutcha*: unmetalled surfaces that are not hard and are usually made of earth, gravel, or sand

life. She would wake up late in the mornings just in time to scramble to school and, upon returning, help her mother with the household work. Shalu would make rotis, clean their little house, and even help Sheela clean other houses. Her father, Mahesh, worked away from their village and was often not at home. The task of managing home and children fell squarely upon Sheela's diffident shoulders, and she was careful to ensure that her children, particularly the girls, did nothing to provoke gossip in the village.

Shalu was very young when PANI set up its resource centre in Pichaura. She would join the girls of her village at the centre three times a week to play games, read books, and participate in discussions that provoked her to think about the possibilities of who she could be. The conversations combined with the games helped her recognise that her passion for games ran deeper than mere play. She decided that she would like to work and wanted to pursue a career in sports. It was an unconventional choice, but Shalu was fortunate to find an avid champion in her father. As a young boy, Mahesh had enjoyed playing cricket and even nursed hopes of becoming a professional sportsman. But he had been married at the tender age of ten and become a father before he turned twenty. Forced to provide for his young family, Mahesh had no choice but to sacrifice his passion for cricket. The regret on his face when he talks of his thwarted dreams is palpable. "I could not follow my passion for sports," he says wistfully, "but I am happy my daughter has opportunities that I did not have and is able to do what I could not."

Sheela, however, was not happy with Shalu's interest in sports. When Shalu started rising at the crack of dawn every day to cycle through the dark, lonely village roads to Tarun, Sheela worried it would take a toll on her daughter's health. More importantly, Sheela feared that the villagers would see Shalu in her training gear and gossip would flare like wildfire. Despite Sheela's worried warnings and admonitions, Mahesh decided to allow Shalu the freedom to follow her dreams. She was allowed to trade her salwars for tracksuits, shorts, and T-shirts, even when she was off the field, and she was often excused from household chores to focus on her studies and training.

In Pichaura, it was unusual for a family to prioritise a daughter's needs and ambitions over their sons'. Mahesh's pride in Shalu and his enthusiastic support for her goals started to change the fabric of their small family. Shalu's older brother found himself lending a hand with the household chores so that Shalu was able to dedicate time to her studies and training. At times, he would even join the womenfolk in cooking a meal. Every time the siblings squabbled, Shalu would scamper off to complain to Mahesh, who would in turn scold his son. "When it comes to sports, it is Papa who supports me the most," Shalu says, her voice ringing with love for her father. "My brother is proud of me, but he also teases me. Whenever we fight, Papa scolds Bhaiya, who then complains that I am the boss of our home." The glee on her face as she describes her skirmishes with her brother is likely to make you smile as you marvel at the transformation of a quiet girl who once had no dreams into a determined athlete who yearns to bring home an Olympic medal one day.

Being a sportsperson has changed Shalu's life, and she is quick to acknowledge it. "I am more disciplined and focused now. When I am on the field, I assess other runners and aim to outrun them. There are times when I feel unnerved by girls who are bigger than me, but I do not let it affect my running," she shares quietly. "I can see that I have become a leader. I train the girls in the absence of our coach, and at home I encourage my sister to focus on her studies and play games rather than do the household chores that I once did." Shalu is currently pursuing her bachelor's degree in physical education and sports. Her ambition is to become an international athlete and then eventually a sports coach who can help many more girls from villages across Uttar Pradesh make their mark in the world of sports. "We reap as we sow," she intones wisely. "I run to win. If I commit to working hard and consistently, then why won't I reap the fruits of my hard work? I too can be an Olympian," she states with conviction.

# 23

## Standing Up for Me

Marriage had been a constant theme in Tara's life right from childhood. She comes from a large, conservative family of farmers in Dhamhar village, who firmly believed in marrying girls young. And yet, Tara had an independent bent of mind at a young age and yearned to work, even if it meant leaving her home and village. "Every girl needs to stand on her feet before she even thinks about marriage," she shares solemnly. "It is important for us to do something in life, and we must stand up for it."

She dared not voice this out loud to her parents or her grandparents. Tara's grandfather, who was the patriarch of the family, had very conservative ideas about how women and girls should conduct themselves. He expected his granddaughters to speak softly, be modestly dressed in salwars, and most importantly, not be seen by men who were not of their family. The segregation rules in their home were so strict that the girls were not even allowed to appear before male guests to serve chai and refreshments. Tara and her sisters therefore did not enjoy much freedom, especially as adolescents. "We were not allowed out much. We did not have the time or the permission," Tara remembers. "If we were seen playing outside, we would be scolded by family members or the villagers. They would tell us that we were no longer small children and cannot be playing or roaming outside the house."

For Tara's grandfather, his granddaughters' education was not a priority. But her father, Chaituram, was willing to let Tara study until the tenth standard. She was allowed to go to school only in the company of other girls. Back then, not many girls in Dhamhar went to school, and there were days when Tara had to miss school for want of company. When PANI opened its resource centre in Dhamhar, Tara found herself drawn to the centre and its activities. Her family, however, viewed the centre with disdain and disapproval. The men in her family would often deride the girls they saw at the centre for speaking too much and for being too bold. When Tara evinced interest in the centre and expressed her desire to visit, both Chaituram and his son were alarmed. They worried that she would be influenced by the girls they saw and sternly prohibited her from visiting.

Jyoti Upadhyay, who managed PANI's centres in the area and was often in Dhamhar, distinctly remembers the draconian controls that Tara had to circumvent when she started visiting the centre. "Tara's younger brother proved to be an impediment," she recalls. "He would mock the girls at the centre for wearing pants and playing games, and taunt Tara for wanting to join them. He would tell her that it was inevitable that she would also start dressing like them and then be harassed by the boys in the village until she cried." Despite her brother's acrid warnings about bringing dishonour to him and their father, Tara refused to give up. Both she and Jyoti persisted and their constant, consistent efforts finally paid off when her family was persuaded.

Chaituram reluctantly granted permission for Tara to visit the centre provided she was accompanied by other girls. Tara, however, enjoyed her visits so much that she would quietly sneak off by herself on the rare occasion she did not have company, knowing full well that she would be mercilessly beaten once the family knew. This was a time when Tara's family was proactively looking to marry her off. She had completed her tenth standard and had enrolled in intermediate school. Her family did not have money to cover her educational expenses and felt marriage was a better option for Tara.

Much to her dismay, her family started to receive marriage proposals and offers for potential alliances almost every day. When Jyoti and the girls at the centre saw Tara crying bitterly, they decided to intervene and tried persuading her parents to hold off on the wedding plans until Tara completed her intermediate schooling. But it was impossible for them to convince her grandfather, who was determined to marry her off as soon as possible. Tara's grandfather did not approve of the permission she had to visit the centre. He was concerned that she would draw unwanted attention from the village boys during her visits and bring dishonour to their family. Fortunately, Jyoti's earnest pleas prevailed and Chaituram grudgingly agreed to defer Tara's marriage until she completed her intermediate schooling.

Despite her family's determination to marry her off and the ensuing drama, Tara had made up her mind to work. She saw her opportunity to pursue this goal when she started participating in discussions about skills development and employability that were frequently held at the resource centre. As she neared completion of her intermediate schooling, Tara decided to be brave and put her name forward for an electrical skills development course, knowing that her family would be very displeased with her. Tara's family was incensed. They decided to conduct her marriage as soon as possible, overriding her vociferous objections and tearful pleas to let her go to Ayodhya for her skills development course. Her argumentativeness and determination to study and work convinced them that they were right in hastening her marriage. They felt she was already too outspoken, too bold, and too independent to be able to settle into a marriage and they feared if she was allowed to leave her home and village under the pretext of studies, it was very likely that she would choose to marry someone of her choice rather than abide by her family's approval. Tara once again leaned in for support from Jyoti and the centre's team.

When Jyoti visited the family, she found that Chaituram and his wife were unwilling to consider the idea of Tara studying any further or working. They were certain that Tara's persistent stand against marriage as well as her insistence upon studying further was due to the disruptive influence of the girls at the centre. Jyoti was hard pressed to explain to Chaituram that Tara was chafing to do more in life than marry and keep house. She wanted to live a good life and, in doing so, support her family. It was through repeated conversations and persuasion that Jyoti was finally able to convince Tara's parents. When Tara completed the electrical skills development course in Ayodhya, she secured a job in Noida through the institute's campus placement centre.

Finally, at twenty, Tara's dreams have started to come true. Today, she works with a good company in the city and contributes a third of her family income. Despite her fight for freedom and to stand on her feet, Tara has struggled to transition into her life as a working girl in the city. The concrete city with its packed buildings, bustling traffic, and overwhelming noise was a rude shock after the rustic calm, the green fields, and vast spaces of the village. Food and water were not as easily available and the hostel she stayed at had rules she had to abide by. Freedom for a girl, she realised, was relative to the place she was in. Back in the village, the controls of her family and the scrutiny of her neighbours made it impossible for her to step out without comments or consequences. But in the city, while people still stared at her, she has the freedom to work, earn, wear the clothes she wants to, and go out within reasonable hours. She can stand up for herself and is happy for now.

# 24

## A Different Cup of Tea

*Princi's prowess on the cricketing field proves to the villagers that girls can do so much more than keep house and make chai.*

The first things you would notice about nineteen-year-old Princi are her twinkling eyes and the upturned corners of her mouth. It is as if she is silently laughing at a delicious joke. Her impish mirth invites you to lean in and ask if she will share her secret with you. Be warned, for if you do ask, she is likely to consider you carefully for a full minute before drench-ing you in a gale of giggles as she declares, "Don't ask me for chai because I do not know how to make it." It is only then that the significance of her pause sinks in. In a country where chai is synonymous with hospitality, it is sacrilegious for a young village girl from Uttar Pradesh to not know how to brew tea.[46]

Princi had always been a different cup of tea from the girls in Mahrai Mohammadpur village. As the youngest born daugh-ter, she was greatly indulged by her father, Birbali Yadav, and her older siblings. Most girls in Mahrai Mohammadpur came home from school to do chores and work in the family's fields. If they had time, they would either play Ludo or sit quietly in a hidden corner of their house.[47] Princi, on the other hand, would round up her brothers and the younger village boys and set out to play cricket. She was perhaps the only girl in Mahrai Mohammadpur who would be seen playing outdoors with the boys in the dead heat of the day.

The people of Mahrai Mohammadpur held conservative ideas about how girls should dress and behave in public. At first, the villagers made thinly veiled remarks about Princi's unladylike conduct to her father. But Birbali Yadav paid no heed to the criticism and judgement of the villagers, not even when they remarked pointedly about his daughter's unorthodox

---

46  Chai: Indian tea, made by boiling tea leaves with milk, sugar, and spices

47  Ludo: A board game for two to four players, in which players race their tokens from start to finish according to the roll of a single die. Like other cross and circle games, Ludo is derived from the Indian game Pachisi.

penchant for boys' games. This, however, was not the case with her mother, Rama Devi. In villages across eastern Uttar Pradesh where there isn't much food to go around and the plates of the women are the last to be filled, it is gossip that often satiates their hunger. The women of Mahrai Mohammadpur savored gossip as they would a hot, crispy *jalebi*[48] straight out of the local *mithaiwala*'s wok.[49] Princi was a favorite topic of conversation amongst them, and they would often taunt Rama Devi for being a bad mother. Unable to stave off their cutting remarks, Rama Devi would scold Princi and plead with her to stay home. But it was to no avail.

Adolescence caught up with Princi when she was in the seventh standard. It put an end to her cricket games and all the freedoms she had enjoyed as a child. This time, Birbali Yadav was unable to flout village convention or intercede with his wife on Princi's behalf. Rama Devi pointed out to her husband and her youngest daughter that their older girls had never stepped out of the house during adolescence. Princi, therefore, was to stay indoors and help with the household chores. Much to Rama Devi's dismay, although Princi's games and rambles ended, she continued to be indulged by her father and older sisters. Other than helping with a few cursory chores around the house, Princi was neither expected nor taught to cook or keep house. This pleased her immensely because she particularly did not like

---

48 *Jalebi*: a batter-fried, sugar-soaked, squiggle-shaped sweet that is eaten as a snack or dessert across India

49 *Mithaiwala*: a person who makes traditional Indian sweets, confectionary, and desserts

cooking. "I often dissuaded people from coming home because I cannot make a cup of tea," she confesses with a mischievous grin. "If anyone drops in unexpectedly, I tell them there is no one at home to make tea or that they need to wait while I get Didi from next door to make tea." A girl who cannot brew a cup of tea tends to be an anomaly in India. It was inevitable that Princi's disinterest in cooking and household chores would irk the village women who continued to chide the hapless Rama Devi, demanding to know how her youngest daughter would manage once she was married. When Rama Devi complained about Princi at home, Birbali Yadav and their older daughters would tell her to let Princi be.

Princi was excited when PANI opened its resource centre in Mahrai Mohammadpur. The prospect of escaping her mother's strict rules and having the freedom to step out of the house was tantalizing. She became a regular visitor at the centre, and soon forged a bond with Sudha Tiwari, who managed a cluster of PANI's resource centres in the region. Sudha was like yet another older sister for Princi. She provoked Princi to think beyond the traditional mould and encouraged her to play to her heart's content. Spotting an opportunity to pursue her passion for cricket once more, Princi decided to muster the village girls and form a cricket team. It was an ambitious and formidable plan. In villages like Mahrai Mohammadpur, cricket is a man's sport and deemed unsuitable for women, who are held to be physically weaker than men. Princi, however, was determined and decided that if tradition would not permit her to play cricket with the boys, she would form a team of girls and play.

She decided to first approach the girls she had once seen playing outside their houses and coax them to try their hand at cricket. Many of the girls she spoke to had doubts and reservations. They also did not know how to play the game. Princi patiently taught them the rudiments of the game, cheering them on as they slowly started to break through their limiting beliefs about what girls can and cannot do. "People in my village do not permit girls to play cricket because they do not see it as a game for boys and girls," she explains candidly. "When we started to play, I found that girls are quick learners. As they started to challenge their belief that cricket is a boys' game, they started playing with confidence and soon were playing well."

Princi's talent and passion soon secured her a spot in PANI's under-19 girls cricket team. All at once, she found herself playing in competitive matches. The change from the village playgrounds to competitive pitches was one she was not quite prepared for. When she thinks back to her first match, she cannot help but laugh at how intimidated she had been by the fast bowling of the opposing team. She soon learnt that "match nerves" came with the pitch, and with each match she played, she would challenge her beliefs about her capabilities and her self-confidence would improve exponentially.

Princi's most memorable matches were the ones she played at the 30th Junior UP Tennis Ball Cricket Association Tournament in Haridwar, where PANI's under-19 girls cricket team clinched the second runners-up place. "The tournament was both exciting and unnerving," she recalls. "There were so many teams and some of the players seemed older than nineteen. Their size and stature made us wonder if we would be able to hold our own against them on the field." But, as her team triumphantly lifted their trophy, Princi realised that the only thing that mattered on the field is a player's game. "Not the size, but the game" is a mantra Princi now uses to ground herself on the pitch day after day. She believes it will enable her to become a well-known cricketer who, one day, will represent India on pitches across the world. She hopes that will be the day when the people of Mahrai Mohammadpur will embrace the truth that young girls, just like chai, come in many different flavors and can thrive if allowed to.

# 25

## A Bride's Rebellion

Who does not love an Indian wedding?

The music and the singing, the food, the dress-ups, the rituals and the dancing, the fun and games, the raucous, happy masses of people, and most importantly, the glittering bride and groom who smile awkwardly at people and cameras as they look forward to a new life together. In India, everyone loves a wedding. Except when the bride is a reluctant nineteen-year-old forced to marry a man twenty years her senior for a princely bride price. Most girls would cry and complain in this situation. But eventually, they would allow themselves to be coerced in the interest of their family's honour. Shalu, however, is not like most girls. As much as her heart ached for her family's struggles with poverty, she refused to marry an unsuitable man, choosing to brave her parents' wrath to build a life for herself on her terms.

Shalu had lived in Jajwara village for most of her life. Her father, Rajbahadur, was the sole earning member in the family and eked out a meagre living as a laborer. Being the eldest of four siblings, Shalu was privy to her parents' struggles in providing for their family and it made her yearn for financial stability. As a young child, she would talk about joining the army when she grew up. It was an audacious dream, even for a girl so young. But poverty made Shalu determine that, one day, she would earn enough money to support her family, hopefully by serving her country.

Her parents, however, dismissed her words as a child's mindless prattle. Like many in the village, they believed that young girls needed to learn to be good homemakers. Shalu was, therefore, raised with little to no freedom. "I never could wear the clothes I wanted nor go out much," she remembers of her early teens. "I would go to school and come home to cook, clean, and finish household chores. There wasn't even time to play." Speaking to boys was taboo. If a boy was to direct a question, comment, or a joke at her, Shalu would be severely scolded and even beaten. The fear of being scolded made her bend her head every time she stepped out and scurry back home as soon as she could.

Shalu dropped out when she was in high school. The family's financial situation had deteriorated to the point where Rajbahadur could no longer afford to educate her. She was now almost fully confined to her house and chafed with restlessness. It was at this juncture that PANI set up its resource centre in Jajwara. Shalu was delighted when Sima Verma and Jameel Ahmad came calling at her home to invite her and her sisters to the centre. Despite having discontinued her education, Shalu still nursed hopes of working at a paying job one day and found herself drawn to Sima's plans to empower adolescent girls in Jajwara. She started visiting the resource centre where she would participate in conversations about her rights, speaking up for herself and making empowering life decisions.

Encouraged by the support, Shalu decided to avail herself of the resources offered by PANI's Back to School programme and resume her schooling. Her parents, however, were skeptical. "The family was suspicious when we spoke to them about permitting Shalu to resume her schooling," remembers Jameel with a wry smile. "They could not understand why we would be willing to fund their daughter's education and questioned our motives. We had to meet them repeatedly to allay their suspicions before Shalu was allowed to resume her studies." However, Shalu's happiness was short lived. Driven by abject poverty, Rajbahadur and his wife Rajkumari decided to marry Shalu off. The husband they found for her was thirty-five years old and lived far away in Rajasthan. Neither the age difference nor the prospect of sending their daughter all the way across North India mattered to them because of the generous bride price they were promised. All at once, Shalu found herself caught in a flurry of wedding preparations that she neither wanted nor asked for. "I was only nineteen years old and not ready for marriage," she shares, her voice betraying her hurt.

"He was so much older than me. I told him I wanted to study and was told that my job after marriage was to serve him and his family." Dismayed by the turn of events, Shalu protested, knowing that her parents could throw her out of the house if she refused to comply with the decision they had made for her. "I kept telling my parents that I would not get married if they accepted the money," she shares. "But they are poor and would not listen to me."

As the wedding date drew closer, Shalu found herself becoming increasingly desperate. She tried talking to her mother about enrolling in a skills development course and getting a job, citing examples of other girls like her who were working and supporting their families. But her parents would not listen. The only people who sympathised with Shalu were her friends at the PANI centre. "Those were stressful times for all of us," recalls Jameel. "We knew there would be harsh consequences if she refused to get married. We wanted to make sure that she was very sure of her decisions. Until then, no one had asked her about what *she* wanted. So, we did. We showed her the two choices she had: marriage or studies and work. She was determined to work." With fifteen days to go and no other recourse in sight, Shalu knew she had to stand up for herself and act. The wedding invitations had been printed and the bride price paid when Shalu, with the support of her friends from the centre, decided to call off the wedding.

It was a scandal that rocked Jajwara to the very last person. Never in the history of the village had a young girl called off her wedding. Shalu's decision infuriated Rajbahadur. He felt his daughter had disgraced herself and brought great dishonour to him. Believing that he had irreparably lost face in the village, Rajbahadur turned his ire on Shalu's mother, blaming her for Shalu's arrogance, disobedience, and the breakdown of the marriage alliance. In their rage, her parents ordered Shalu to leave the house.

Fortunately, Shalu's grandparents were sympathetic and took her in. Over the next few months, Shalu lived with them and continued her education. By the time she finished her intermediate schooling, her parents were calmer and willing to listen to her plans. They believed she was disgraced beyond redemption and would not be able to make a good marriage anymore. So when Shalu spoke to them about enrolling in a skills development programme with PANI's support, they agreed. It was thus that Shalu found herself training to be an electrician in Faizabad.

Today, Shalu lives in Delhi, India's capital city, and works in retail sales at a mall. Unlike many girls from villages who struggle to adjust to living independently in a big city, Shalu thrives. "People told me that Delhi is unsafe for young women. They told me that I can be killed and thrown into the gutter," she says. "At first, I was scared and felt I would not be able to live by myself. But I decided that if I am okay with myself, then all else will be okay. Now, I live alone and travel by myself. I work, earn, and do things by myself. I have no fear now because I can live without being controlled and restricted by others."

Shalu's road to freedom has been long and arduous. But it was worth the fight. "I learnt that if I stand on my feet, then no one can tell me anything," she shares with conviction. "If I am financially dependent on another, then I am at their mercy. In my house, if my mother spends a rupee, she must account for it to my father.[50] Watching my mother have no freedom to make simple purchases made me want to stand on my feet." The life Shalu leads today, and the financial support she offers to her family, has allayed her parent's reservations. They are encouraging of her ambitions now and tell her she can marry whomever she wants, whenever. She has come a long way from being the bride whose defiance shocked a village.

But what lies ahead for her now?

She has big dreams for herself and her family.

She wants to build them a nice home to live in.

She wants to educate her sisters.

She wants to travel and work in different cities.

She wants to learn new skills and become a department store manager.

The world is her oyster, for she knows no fear.

---

50  Rupee: The Indian currency is referred to as the Indian rupee. Much like the dollar, the rupee is also a basic monetary unit.

## Epilogue

# Fanning the Winds of Change

The stories in this book are more than just journeys of adolescent girls in villages defying parental and familial restrictions. They are markers of the larger changes that have transformed the very landscape of the Tarun block in Ayodhya district.

You will be able to witness this for yourself if your path ever winds past this region. As you drive through, you will see girls in shorts cycling furiously towards their training grounds, schools, or back to their home. You will see them dressed in pants, walking confidently on the dusty, broken roads, like they belong.

They are a startling contrast to the neighbouring blocks where the girls are still mostly invisible and yearn for the same opportunities, empowerment, and freedom.

The stories you have read are a clarion call to extend the reach of these changes and transform young lives beyond the boundaries of Tarun. It is now time for us to glean the wisdom from our journey with the girls of Tarun and apply our learnings on a larger scale.

Our mission has two primary objectives.

Firstly, we aim to identify the scalable elements from our experiences in Tarun and use them as building blocks for broader systemic change. This involves reimagining the structures, systems, policies, and societal norms that have relegated girls to the backseat for far too long. We seek to create long-term, sustainable progress across wider regions.

Secondly, as we expand horizontally, we aim to touch more lives, retaining our commitment to delving deeper into the disempowering challenges that beset the girls of Tarun.

While progress has been made, true equality still seems like a distant ideal in many aspects of their lives. We acknowledge that this is a complex task that demands sustained efforts over the long term.

But we are unwavering in our commitment and envision these girls as the instruments of change.

Their resilience, determination, and unwavering spirit have already transformed the face of Tarun.

Now, it is time to fan that flame to spread the warmth of progress across Uttar Pradesh and beyond.

We invite you to join us on this journey.

The winds of change are blowing strong in Tarun.

The time is right for us to let it catch our wings and carry us onward to a brighter, more equitable future for all.

# Acknowledgements

*Happy Shiny People: the didis and bhaiyas
of PANI who help the girls splash and ripple change.*

*Top row, left to right: Jagdish Giri, Meenakshi Dwivedi, Udai Tiwari,
Roopwati, Shailesh Tiwari, Mr. Dharmendra Kumar, Mr. Manish Singh;
middle row, left to right: Vikram Veer Singh, Anjali Pandey, Vineet Kumar
Singh, Sima Verma, Sudha Tiwari, Rajendra Prasad Tiwari;
bottom row, left to right: Archana Chaturvedi, Shyam Bahadur Verma,
Jyoti Upadhyay, Jameel Ahmad, Kamlawati*

W e acknowledge the unstinting efforts of the women and men of PANI who have worked diligently and relentlessly to educate, counsel, and support the girls and their families in paving new empowering paths for themselves, their sisters, peers, and future generations of girls in the region.

We acknowledge and express our gratitude to our partners, consultants, and trainers who have helped us shape our different programmes and contributed to their effectiveness.

We record our appreciation and thankfulness to the government officials at the block level, the Gram Pradhans, village communities, and the parents of every girl in our programmes.

We express our gratitude to the teams at Greenleaf Book Group and BrainTrust Ink for their enthusiastic support for this book and their generous partnership for its publication.

# Glossary

**Agarbatti:** incense or joss sticks; thin, wooden sticks coated in a fragrant mixture of herbs, resins, and oils, and burnt for fragrance

**Ammi:** mother; the proper noun or form of address for "mother" in Urdu and a few other Indian languages

**Anthakshari:** a popular singing game in India

**Bade Papa:** a paternal uncle who is older to one's father

**Bhabhi:** sister-in-law; the proper noun or form of address for the older sister-in-law, in Hindi and many other Indian languages

**Bhaiya, Bhai:** older brother; the proper noun or form of address for elder brother, elder cousin, or an older man in Hindi and many other Indian languages

**Bhajans:** a devotional song in any language, which has a religious theme or spiritual ideas and is sung at temples and spiritual gatherings

**Bollywood:** the Indian popular film industry, based in Mumbai

**Chacha, Chachaji:** uncle; a proper noun or form of address for a father's younger brother in Hindi and many other Indian languages

**Chai:** Indian tea, made especially by boiling tea leaves with milk, sugar, and spices

**Charpai:** a traditional four-legged woven bed that is used for sitting or lying during the day and for sleeping at night

**Chauraha:** crossroads

**Chulha:** a traditional U-shaped mud cooking stove used for indoor cooking in villages

**Dadi:** paternal grandmother; the proper noun or form of address for the paternal grandmother in Hindi and many other Indian languages

**Dada, Dadaji, Dadu:** paternal grandfather; the proper noun or form of address for the paternal grandfather in Hindi and many other Indian languages

**Dhol:** a double-headed barrel drum that is widely used, with regional variations, in many parts of India

**Dholi:** someone who plays the dhol

**Didi:** older sister; the proper noun or form of address for older sister, older female cousin, or an older woman in Hindi and many other Indian languages

**Dupatta:** a long, shawl-like scarf traditionally worn by women on the Indian subcontinent to cover the head, face, and upper body

**Gram panchayat, Panchayat:** village council; a basic governing institution (political) in Indian villages, acting as the village's cabinet

**Gully:** colloquial reference to the alleys and streets between houses where children play

**Gully Cricket:** roughly translates to street cricket

**Hindi:** One of India's twenty-two official languages that is popularly spoken across North India. India has over 120 major languages and more than 1,500 dialectic variations.

**Item Number:** A musical performance that is often inserted into an Indian movie to entertain or increase its market value. It usually is catchy and tends to come with a sensual dance sequence.

**Jaebi:** a batter-fried, sugar-soaked, squiggle-shaped sweet that is eaten as a snack or dessert across India

**Jan Sewa Kendra:** "A Centre That Serves People"

**Kabaddi:** a contact team sport of Indian origin played by teams of seven on a circular court, where players attempt to tag their opponents while repeating the word "kabaddi"

**Kirana stores:** small mom-and-pop grocery and general supplies stores found in neighbourhoods

**Kutcha:** unmetalled surfaces that are not hard and usually made of earth, gravel, or sand.

**Langoti:** loincloth; a narrow strip of cloth passed between the legs and fastened before and behind to a string around the waist, usually worn by men and boys

**Lobia beans:** black-eyed beans, black-eyed peas, cow peas

**Ludo:** a board game for two to four players, in which players race their tokens from start to finish according to the rolls of a single die

**Mistri:** a foreman or supervisor of manual workers in India

**Mithaiwala:** a person who makes traditional Indian sweets, confectionary, and desserts

**Moti:** a fat woman or girl

**Mukhiya:** village headman

**Nag Panchami:** a festival dedicated to the snake gods, or the nagas, that occurs on the first day after the new moon in the month of Shravan

**Nana:** maternal grandfather; the proper noun or form of address for the maternal grandfather in Hindi and many other Indian languages

**Nani:** maternal grandmother; the proper noun or form of address for the maternal grandmother, in Hindi and many other Indian languages

**Puja:** ritualistic worship of gods; widely used in most major Indian languages to refer to the ritualistic worship performed daily at home, in temples, in offices, and in public spaces during festivals

**Raag:** a piece of Indian classical music based on a traditional scale or pattern of notes

**Raaginiyan:** a piece of Indian classical music based on a traditional scale or pattern of notes

**Roti:** Indian unleavened flatbread that is usually cooked over a griddle

**Rupee:** The Indian currency is referred to as the Indian rupee. Much like the dollar, the rupee is also a basic monetary unit.

**Salwar Kameez/Salwar Suit:** a type of suit worn especially by South Asian women, with loose trousers [salwar] and a long shirt/tunic [kameez]

**Shravan:** a holy month in the lunar-based Hindu calendar which is marked by fasting, prayers, and religious festivals.

# About the Author and PANI

**REKHA SALEELA NAIR** leverages two decades of experience in corporate branding and communications, radio, and advertising to partner with her clients to take their leadership and executive careers to the next level. A trained transactional analysis practitioner, Rekha provides consultation and coaching to help clients overcome limiting beliefs and behavioural patterns to articulate authentic, results-oriented personal/professional brands resulting in increased leadership credibility and business results. Raised in a matrilineal Indian family by women who role-modeled leadership in their communities, Rekha specialises in coaching women to smash through their inner ceilings, build their confidence, and increase their impact with respect and compassion.

Rekha served as head of corporate communications at Dynamatic Technologies Limited, an Indian engineering multinational corporation that operates in the hydraulics, automotive, and aerospace domains. As custodian of the corporate brand, she was an integral part of the executive leadership team that spearheaded the company's growth from a ₹100 crores single-domain Indian business to a ₹1800 crores multidomain, multigeographic entity. During her fifteen-year tenure, she successfully translated complex business information into authentic, high-impact strategic branding and communications initiatives for diverse business situations in India, Europe, and the US. These included mergers and acquisitions, crises communications, CSR, investor and shareholder relations, as well as collaborative initiatives with global primes like Boeing, Airbus, and Bell Helicopters.

Rekha is the founder of Dragonflies Everywhere, an Indian registered nonprofit that supports the work of nonprofit leaders serving grassroots communities in Africa and South Asia through volunteered coaching and mentoring around leadership, management, communication, storytelling, brand development, and other key areas for success. Rekha is frequently invited by international MNCs, colleges, and NGOs to speak about personal branding at their leadership and DEI programmes.

**People's Action For National Integration (PANI)**

PANI, a social organisation based in northern India, is dedicated to crafting transformative and sustainable solutions for global challenges such as poverty, inequality, and climate change. Our strategic approach revolves around empowering individuals and communities with the knowledge and skills required to actively address these challenges.

With a dynamic and empathetic multidisciplinary team, PANI collaborates with governments, organisations, and local communities to implement initiatives focused on poverty alleviation, empowerment of women and girls, health and nutrition improvement, and environmental sustainability. Our mission is clear: contribute to the creation of a more equitable and resilient world.

Founded in 1986 by a group of committed Gandhian social activists, the organisation embodies Gandhian principles of rural reconstruction and nation-building with people's actions at its core. We believe in the inherent agency of people to drive the change they need.

Over nearly four decades, PANI has directly impacted the lives of more than 2.5 million households in the states of Uttar Pradesh, Himachal Pradesh, Rajasthan, and Bihar. Through initiatives that promote awareness, education, and self-determination, PANI remains unwavering in enabling communities to take greater control of their lives and drive positive change in the world around them.

www.ingramcontent.com/pod-product-compliance
Lightning Source LLC
Chambersburg PA
CBHW031510120626
46545CB00005B/1811

* 9 781956 072211 *